MEDIEVAL CHRISTIAN
PHILOSOPHY

IS VOLUME

12

OF THE

Twentieth Century Encyclopedia of Catholicism

UNDER SECTION

I

KNOWLEDGE AND FAITH

IT IS ALSO THE

45TH

VOLUME IN ORDER OF PUBLICATION

Edited by HENRI DANIEL-ROPS of the Académie Française

MEDIEVAL CHRISTIAN PHILOSOPHY

By PHILIPPE DELHAYE

Translated from the French by S. J. TESTER

HAWTHORN BOOKS · PUBLISHERS · *New York*

First Edition, July, 1960
Second Printing, March, 1963

NIHIL OBSTAT

Adrianus van Vliet, S.T.D.

Censor Deputatus

IMPRIMATUR

E. Morrogh Bernard

Vicarius Generalis

Westmonasterii, die XI APRILIS MCMLX

CONTENTS

INTRODUCTION

Almost every word in the title, "Medieval Christian Philosophy," can be argued about.

CHRISTIAN PHILOSOPHY

It is not our concern here to take up again the problem of Christian philosophy: M. Nédoncelle has dealt with it in masterly fashion in another volume in this series.[1] Nevertheless, we must call the reader's attention to the way this expression developed, and consequently to the meaning it ought to have within the medieval conception of knowledge.

As a modern phrase, "Christian philosophy" is difficult to explain, for philosophy is a strictly natural discipline appealing to the light of reason alone, while the Christian faith accepts revelation as the principle and the first criterion of reflective thought, and holds that theology unfolds the meaning of what is revealed, or draws conclusions from it, by reasonable, reflective methods. So, in the strict sense of the terms, Christian philosophy and Scholastic theology would be the same thing, since in both cases the starting point is a dogma of faith and the means of investigation a reasoning process using philosophical ideas to throw light on the faith. Now it is indeed quite clear that it is not this that modern supporters or exponents of Christian philosophy have wanted to put forward. When Pope Leo XIII used the phrase in the encyclical *Aeterni Patris*, in the title itself, he intended to recommend a genuine philosophy, but one which was not closed to but consistent with Christianity and took its teachings into account. It was in

[1] M. Nédoncelle, *Is there a Christian Philosophy?*, in this series. Much relevant bibliographical information will also be found in G. A. de Brie, *Bibliographica philosophica*, 1939-45, vol. 2 (Antwerp, 1954); Nos. 24.246-24.336.

this sense that Jacques Maritain said that the faith is an extrinsic criterion of true philosophy: if the philosopher arrives at conclusions contrary to the teaching of the Church he must consider himself mistaken and go back over his arguments. But he must leave to the theologian the duty and privilege of accepting as principles or as essential elements in his arguments the data of revelation. Or to take another author, for these are only examples, Blondel called a philosophy Christian, or better Catholic, if it was aware of its own insufficiency and was open to revelation, to which in a vague way it appealed or which it at least knew it needed.

The medieval meaning, medieval ideas, are quite different. Although at that time the word "philosophers" (*philosophi*) meant almost exclusively the thinkers of pagan antiquity, the word "philosophy" had a much wider significance, making it equivalent to wisdom, knowledge, manner of life, view of the world. It was therefore quite legitimate to speak of Christian philosophy when what was meant was Christian wisdom, a manner of living and thinking genuinely Christian even though it also appealed to the use of the reason. The scholars of the Middle Ages read a good deal of St Augustine, and knew texts in which he declared Christianity to be the true philosophy: "Believe me, pagan philosophy is no better than our Christian philosophy, which is the only true philosophy, since by this name is meant zeal for or love of wisdom; for see what Cicero says in his *Hortensius*. . . ."[2]

Boëthius and St Isidore of Seville, for whom the ages that followed had the greatest veneration, had the same idea of

---

[2] St Augustine, *Contra Julianum*, 4, 72; Migne, *Patrologia Latina* (hereafter quoted as Migne, *P.L.* followed by volume and column number), 44, col. 774: *obsecro te, non sit honestior philosophia gentium quam nostra christiana, quae una est vera philosophia, quandoquidem studium vel amor sapientiae significatur hoc nomine. Vide enim quid in Hortensii dialogo dicat Tullius....* St Augustine here suggests a syllogism: Cicero defined philosophy as the love of wisdom; but Christianity is the love of wisdom at its highest; therefore it is the highest philosophy. See, in the same sense, *De civ. Dei*, 10, 32; 22, 22: *P.L.*, 41, 312 and 787.

philosophy. When, in the twelfth century, Hugh of St Victor wanted to define philosophy he reproduced the very words of Boëthius: philosophy is the love of and search for wisdom, and especially it is the love of God.[3] Taking up again the Platonic idea of philosophy as the meditation on death, Hugh said, following St Isidore of Seville, that this was much more the action of Christians than of pagans (op. cit., 2, 1).

In the following century St Thomas, although much more careful about differences in method and the distinction of the realms of reason and faith, did not hesitate to identify wisdom and philosophy. In his commentary on Aristotle's Metaphysics (1, 3, 56) he remarks that the two terms are equivalent. Pythagoras, and Aristotle after him, preferred the second because it carried with it a feeling of humility and of impartiality: to say that one is a philosopher is to say that one is a lover and seeker of wisdom for its own sake, with no thought for the advantages it might bring.

In this sense, then, the Christian philosophy of the medieval thinkers is part of their teaching on God, man and the world. They expressed their manner of looking at each of these subjects without always clearly distinguishing the theological and philosophical aspects, in the sense in which we moderns, being different, understand these terms. We must therefore deal with

[3] Hugh of St Victor, *Didascalicon*, 1, 2; ed. Buttimer, p. 6–7. As against this, in Hugh's writings the name "theology" still refers to a pagan or philosophical discipline, the mythology of Varro or Plato's metaphysics (*ibid.*, 2, 2; 3, 2; pp. 25, 49). In the twelfth century what we call theology was called *pagina sacra, sacra doctrina, or divinitas*. Purely as a matter of interest, notice that the Middle Ages were to go so far as to give the name "Christian philosophy" to monasticism, the highest expression of the life of wisdom. To the texts cited by Du Cange may be added those gathered together by Dom Jean Leclercq, *Pour l'histoire de l'expression "philosophie chrétienne"*, in *Mélanges de Science religieuse*, 1952, pp. 221–6. Cassiodorus, in his *Historia ecclesiastica tripartita*, 1, 11 (*CSEL*, vol. 71, pp. 33–43) draws an extended parallel between philosophy and the monastic life. Sometimes the phrase "Christian philosophy" became synonymous with "Christianity", as in the chronicler cited by Du Cange under *philosophia* in his *Glossarium mediae et infimae latinitatis: Otokarus dux ... arma in Prussiam movit, crucesignatus terrae maximam partem Philosophiam Christianam recipere vi coegit....*

them, and study them, as we study Clement of Alexandria or St Augustine; no one will claim that St Augustine, because he is above all a Christian thinker, did not teach any philosophy, but restricted himself exclusively to the theological field.

From this point of view we may sometimes wonder whether the study of medieval thought has not at times been vitiated by a certain anachronism, or even a certain prejudice which Etienne Gilson characterized with his customary authority:

> For a hundred years the general tendency of historians of medieval thought seems to have been to present the Middle Ages as filled with philosophers rather than theologians.... Since philosophy was established as a discipline explicitly separated from theology in the sixteenth century, it has been thought possible to oppose Scholasticism, as a purely philosophical system, to those other purely philosophical systems that attacked it.... Then as now, it was a matter of setting one philosophy against another; that is why the medieval theologians, who never in their lifetime wrote a single philosophical work, have written so many since their death.... More and more, historical research tends now to set their philosophical thought back in its proper place in the theology that contained it.[4]

In this primary meaning, which is demanded by the history of medieval thought, Christian philosophy needs to be studied in its entirety, both in its theological and its philosophical aspects, in the modern sense of these words. Systematically to exclude the theological aspect would be to give a garbled account of the mind of Christendom. Certainly, we are entitled to be more interested in logic or psychology than in controversies on predestination or the Eucharist. But we must not forget that it was the same men, or at any rate the same ideas, that found expression in both. When we study psychology, we cannot remove it altogether from consideration of the thought of the Victorines on the action of grace on the faculties of man. It may be that the contemplative ideal will never be precisely

[4] E. Gilson, *Les recherches historico-critiques et l'avenir de la scholastique*, in *Scholastica ratione historico-critica instaurata: Acta congressus scholastici internationalis Romae anno sancto MCML celebrati* (Rome, 1951), pp. 133–6.

the object of our inquiries, and that we shall here be much more concerned to define the parts played by the imagination, the reason and the understanding. Nothing can be more proper, provided always that we do not divide the two, the philosophical and the theological aspects, in our abstract theorizing, nor conceal what we are leaving out of consideration.

There is another thing which entitles medieval philosophy to the epithet "Christian": the way in which it had to rethink and adapt the great systems of ancient philosophy. Even those who cannot bring themselves to speak of Christian philosophy will readily admit that there is a Christian Aristotelianism and a Christian Platonism.

Here again the problem has quite different forms in modern and in medieval times.

For, since Descartes, the ideal philosophical system is that in which a thinker starts from a first, fundamental idea and builds up a vast system of thought giving an explanation of reality. Perhaps it is contradicted and refuted a few years later; perhaps it depends more on tradition than it thinks or admits. No matter: the system is presented as a new creation, a new departure. Hence philosophical schools play as small a part as possible: the master has his pupils, true, but after the first moment of enthusiasm when it is fitting that they should gather round him, intellectual dependence is not only not important but is even looked upon with disfavour.

In antiquity on the other hand—and the Middle Ages were no different in this regard—the importance of the schools was immense and almost universal. There were a few great schools of thought, like Platonism, Aristotelianism, Stoicism; and to one or other of these belong the great majority of thinkers. None is so bound to his school as to deny himself any originality or exchange of ideas with other systems. But the fundamental theses were accepted; what was doubtful, what was essentially a matter of choice, was firmly established. Whereas we pride ourselves on our independence in our thought, the ancients took pride in being gathered around a

master and continuing his teaching. This, indeed, is how there
came into being a *philosophia perennis*, which had the merit of
providing firm answers to many problems: it constitutes a
privileged foundation for the study of philosophy, for it includes the teachings of so many of the thinkers of the past.
This is one of the reasons why the Church desires that its
clergy should be formed in the philosophy of St Thomas: at
once boldly enterprising and conservative, it gives a specially
rich exposition of this classical philosophy.

It is therefore easily understandable that when we speak of
Christian philosophy in the Middle Ages we are in fact thinking of Christian Platonism and Aristotelianism; for Stoicism
had less influence, except for the ethics of Seneca. This per-
sistence of the ancient systems perhaps also explains how
medieval thought, while being Christian, could still be truly
philosophical. Indeed, if any scholar had wanted to create a
system entirely his own, he would perhaps have been stifled by
the theocratic atmosphere in which he lived. He would have
put forward a doctrine in which only God perhaps had his
accustomed place. In fact, nothing of the sort happened: every
would-be philosopher of the Middle Ages enrolled himself in
the Platonic or Aristotelian tradition, and found in the works
of the masters or their successors an invitation to deal with
philosophical ideas for themselves, to study a logic, a
psychology, a system of metaphysics, even of ethics, all
established before the Gospel had been preached. It is easy
therefore to understand with what eagerness the medieval
scholars searched the works of the ancients and procured translations of them from the Arabic or from the Greek.

Should we say that in these conditions the medieval thinkers
produced bad philosophy or bad theology? This would be true
if they had shown themselves to be mediocre students who
made things more complicated by playing a kind of double
game intellectually. But it was not so. True, they were not all
geniuses. Reading some of them we do sometimes get the
feeling they are dull and shallow. As we recreate the Middle
Ages we must be careful not to fall into a partisan frame of

mind generally analogous in its basic inspiration to that of those who object to them on principle. But why should we dwell on these writers of the second rank any more than we should in giving an account of our own times? The great minds of the Middle Ages were able to enter perfectly into the spirit of the ancient systems, which were thereby enriched. In deductive logic, for example, they carried their analysis so far that twentieth-century logicians refer to their teachings more than to any other. In metaphysics the medieval philosophers carried on Greek thought in identifying Being and God; they nevertheless gave to contingent beings a status and a nature which set them equally far from the world of appearance of Plato and the materialism of Aristotle and the Stoics. They introduced into the very notion of contingency the Biblical idea of time and history that the Greek concept of an eternal world subject to cyclic renewal tended to deny. From this comes the extraordinary agreement of medieval with modern thought on the existential aspect of the world. Only those may be mistaken about this who cannot penetrate the "essential" language which the Middle Ages often took over from the Greeks and preserved just when they were giving it a new meaning. These are only examples which the rest of this book will multiply. The idea to get hold of here is that, even though they were Christians and pupils of the Greeks, the great thinkers of the Middle Ages nevertheless succeeded in creating something entirely their own. What is more, is it not surprising that it is only in its medieval form that Aristotelianism has still its greatest strength? Where does it now survive except in Neo-Scholasticism? Should we say that it has changed? Yes, for it has been a living thing, it has not been simply a matter of empty, parrot-like repetition, but, made alive by contact with another stream of thought, it has been made new.

Here again, to understand things we must set them back in their context. The modern historian of philosophy tries to set out Aristotle's system as faithfully as possible; and he has done as much for St Thomas (though one might wish that he had had more success here). Then he compares the two and is

shocked, if he is an admirer of Aristotle; or on the other hand
he rejoices, if he is glad to be able to show that after all
Thomism is not so Aristotelian as has been claimed. Thomism
seems to be a very stylish system, always dressed in the latest
fashion: it has been presented as rationalist, as essentialist, as
existentialist. If only we could keep it as it is, in its proper,
original nature! In any case it is important to see that the
historian's eye is not that of the philosopher. The former carefully notes the various stages of a process of development; we
might easily say that the formal object of his study is change
and difference. But the philosopher wants to rethink and relive
a system from the inside; he does it as faithfully as he can for
the master of his choice, but he also does it with all the power
of his mind, with his own problems, with his own eye, seeing it
in his way. Above these differences, which are necessary to the
very authenticity of his own work, he is aware of a deep con-
tinuity, of an inward loyalty that enables him to understand
the system he studies in its plenary sense, if I may borrow a
term from contemporary exegesis, itself so aware of the con-
tinuity and of the progress of Biblical studies.

These medieval thinkers, as they looked at the works of the
ancient philosophers, did not feel themselves to be faced by a
system of thought different in kind from Christianity, which
they should indeed make use of, but only as a master con-
descends to use a servant. Their attitude in this was very
different from that of the Fathers, whose consciences were often
troubled when they went back to pagan authors. And we can
understand them: it is not easy to contract, or at any rate to
recognize, a debt to one's enemies. There was vigorous opposition between the Fathers of the Church and the pagans. Things
were not so in the Middle Ages: if there were still pagans, they
were wretched peasants buried in the depths of the forests, no
longer the heirs of Plato and Aristotle. There was thus no need
to keep up a defensive attitude. It was dropped the more readily
since, with that optimism which is characteristic of youth, it
was almost the belief of the Middle Ages that the philosophers
had been more or less inspired by God. This was not, of course,

inspiration like that of the Scriptures, but it was not the less real. Abelard and Hugh of St Victor say as much, bluntly; and St Thomas himself, though infinitely more careful and strict about such theological ideas, when he meets the harshness of St Jerome or St Augustine against the philosophers, studiously distinguishes their basic authority from their errors. St Augustine had said: "If the philosophers produced any truth ... it is to be claimed back from them for our use, as from those who took possession of it illegally".[5] To which St Thomas replies: "The study of philosophy is proper and praiseworthy for itself, because of the truth which the philosophers perceived, for God revealed it to them, as St Paul says in Rom. 1. 19. But because certain of the philosophers misused this truth to attack the faith, St Paul warns us in Coloss. 2. 8: 'Take care not to let anyone cheat you with his philosophizings, with empty phantasies drawn from human tradition, from worldly principles; they were never Christ's teaching'."[6]

Speaking in this way, St Thomas echoes the whole medieval tradition, fighting against the purists of the time to maintain the right of Christians to study the philosophers. Would so much zeal, so much intellectual curiosity, have ended in nothing, in complete failure? It is worth looking at it more closely, and not judging it with the bitter prejudice of the humanists or, worse still, from complete ignorance of the texts.

THE FIVE PERIODS OF THE MIDDLE AGES

The name and the chronological limits of the Middle Ages are also the subject of much discussion. Some put the earlier limit at the death of Theodosius in 395, because it was then that the Western and Eastern Empires finally separated and the Western entered a period of rapid decay. Rome was sacked by Alaric in 410, but already the barbarians were establishing their kingdoms all around. Others prefer the date 476, because it was then that the Gothic king Odoacer deposed the last

[5] *De Doct. Christ.*, II, 40; Migne, *P.L.*, 34, col. 63.
[6] *Summa Theol.*, IIa–IIae, qu. 167, art. 1 ad 3.

Western Emperor Romulus Augustulus and scornfully sent the imperial insignia to Zeno in Constantinople. Others again, like Pirenne, more concerned with economic and cultural history, would see the ancient world as continuing into the seventh century, which saw the western world hemmed in and closed upon itself by the sudden expansion of Islam. All this is of little importance, and one thing is clear: the west passed through a crisis in every field; a new civilization had slowly to be built on the ruins of the ancient world. It was to be wholly spontaneous and new, made by a curious mixing: lovingly preserved and venerated, the elements of the classical world were to be brought to life with a vitality and spontaneity contrasting strongly and happily with the hardening of the arteries of dying antiquity, incapable of renewing itself or of solving the problems it had to face.

There is the same uncertainty about the other limit of this period. It is usually given as 1453, the date of the fall of Constantinople to the Turks. But why look in the east for a dividing date for what concerns the life of the west? It would be more logical to look to the great discoveries (it was in 1498 that Columbus discovered the continent we call America) or to the birth of Protestantism in 1517: the conditions of life, material, moral and intellectual, were then completely changed by this break-up of Christendom.

As is well known, these chronological limits were fixed from the outside by Renaissance men of letters, who wished to forget ten centuries of Europe's history in order to join themselves wholly to the ancient world. The deliberateness of this rejection is marked by the choice of a somewhat scornful term: *media aetas, medium aevum*,[7] as A. Pauphillet has remarked:

> It is part of the fate of the Middle Ages to suggest wrong ideas to modern men. The very name we know them by is a good example. One would suppose that this proper name should refer to an essential unity, to the permanence of some distinctive characteristics: "Middle Ages" should be analogous to "Renais-

[7] Cf. G. L. Burr, "How the Middle Ages got their name", in *American Historical Review*, 18, pp. 710–26; 20, 813.

sance" or "the Age of Enlightenment". Yet, by an odd contrast, this name only defines this period by relation to that which preceded and that which followed, as if its only peculiarity was its place between two more easily definable periods. It is a time between two others, a simple filling-up of the chronological sequence. *Middle* Ages—what is *neither* antiquity *nor* modern times: is not this merely a negation, a region of shadow between two areas of light? There indeed we see the dogmatic disdain of the classical mind.

Under this vague heading are gathered together ten centuries: ten centuries of activity, of political, literary and artistic creation, centuries in which Europe never stopped changing in form and spirit. . . .

In fact, of course, any such collective designation of such diversity is bound to be inadequate. Let us not try to define these ten centuries in three words; but neither let us commit the worse error of thinking they cannot be defined at all. Of all the names that might have been found "the Middle Ages" is surely one of the worst, for it suggests that this time was an obscure passage in the onward march of history, one of unhappy waiting. However, it has become the conventionally accepted name, and as such we shall keep it, though it has no more meaning in itself than an algebraic symbol. We always say that the sun sets, though we no longer believe the childish cosmology the expression implies to be true. So we can still talk of "the Middle Ages", provided we get rid of the ignorance and prejudices formerly attaching to these words.[8]

It seems, then, proper to make clearer than before the differences between the periods into which the Middle Ages can be divided and which show the historical rôle played by the most famous men in each.

The founders of the Middle Ages[9]

This is the period from the end of the fifth to the end of the eighth century. It is that in which the last of the Romans, such as Boëthius and Cassiodorus, still formed in the schools and

[8] A. Pauphillet, *Le Legs du Moyen âge* (Melun, 1950), p. 23.
[9] The phrase is taken from the title of E. K. Rand's book, *The Founders of the Middle Ages* (Harvard Univ. Press, 1928).

universities of the empire, produced a kind of abstract of the knowledge of the ancients. These laymen handed on to the monks their knowledge and their outlines of study. In many regards they remained fixed in pagan ways of thought, but they also treated of theological problems: Boëthius left *The Consolation of Philosophy*, in which the name of Christ does not appear, but he also left his *opuscula sacra*, which were to provide later theologians with subjects for research. These men were also politicians in the service of the barbarian kings: with greater or less success they moved between the two worlds, the ancient and the new.

Their successors as masters of western thought were monks or clerks: St Gregory and St Isidore of Seville. They were confronted with a new situation, for the barbarians were now permanently settled and established. For the Church it was now a matter of converting these barbarians; for the thinkers, of maintaining within this barbarian society the rights of truth and morality. The process began with the baptism of Clovis in 496, but the conversion of Reccared, the Gothic king of Spain, from Arianism to Catholicism did not occur till 589. The conditions in Spain were then such as to bring about that close collaboration between Church and state which was to characterize the whole medieval period. At first, this coalition was marked by the clear predominance of the state, as had been the case under Constantine and was still in the east; the reforms of Gregory VII were to give the supremacy to the papacy.

The great influence of the monks, observing many different rules, especially that of St Columba, was characteristic of this period. Irish and English monks had much to do with the preservation of culture in the west: the name of the Venerable Bede (672–735) is often recalled as a symbol of a very wide learning.

The Carolingian renaissance

This is the second period, characterized by the reforms of Pippin the Short and Charlemagne. These princes wanted, indeed, to restore the habits of study and education not only among the clergy but among laymen also. They were assisted by Italians such as Peter of Pisa and Paulinus of Aquileia, by Irishmen such as Dungal, and by Englishmen like Alcuin. Their efforts succeeded in giving new life to culture in France, and especially in northern France, which up to that time had been deprived of its antique inheritance. We can perhaps see in this the "march of history" which from then on moved towards the supremacy of Paris and its future university. Many of the masters of this period were monks—Benedictine monks, for the emperor had unified the religious observances of his empire. Each monastery generally had a school attached open to clergy and laity.

In many respects the culture of the Carolingian period was simply traditional; only John Scotus Erigena created a system of his own. But besides the classical inheritance we find questions of logic, of metaphysics, of psychology and of ethics being asked and answered at that time. Lastly, these are the "Dark Ages": the first German empire dissolved into the anarchy and chaos of German and Italian states, France was still coming into being, and Spain fell beneath the Arab yoke.

The renaissance of the eleventh and twelfth centuries

This was the period of the restoration of order: the Ottos rebuilt the Empire in Germany, Hugh Capet was elected, on June 1st, 987, "the first of the forty kings who in eight centuries built France", and England was soon to find peace under William the Conqueror. Emperor and kings stood at the head of the feudal system, which brought them the aid—sometimes, it is true, the turbulent aid—of vassals without whom they could never have governed, in an age when responsible leaders were needed in every district. If the peasants took some time to free themselves completely from conditions of servitude, the townsfolk won their independence in the new cities. For the towns were reborn as centres of manufacture, commerce and culture. The sons of the townsmen wanted education; the clergy had to train their new recruits. This is why the canonical schools then became so extraordinarily important. They are so called because they were run by canons, some of whom accepted all the observances of the religious life, while others retained their· private property and some independence but nevertheless performed the Church's ministry as a collegiate body. It was the great age of the cathedral clergy, who, reformed by Gregory VII and his successors, eagerly accepted their teaching duties. We should also observe that alongside of them worked the laymen—and laywomen, who almost everywhere ran schools specially for girls—who, especially in Italy, renewed in their municipal schools the traditions of the public education of antiquity. On the other hand, the monks tended to withdraw from teaching, which they regarded as a secular and profane occupation; this was especially the case for Cluny and Cîteaux.

Then there were the countless urban schools, above all in the country between the Rhine and the Loire. What was taught in them? First and foremost, there were such great works of synthesis as the *De mundi universitate* of Bernard Sylvestris and the *Anticlaudianus* of Alain of Lille. In them, the Bible and Platonism, nature and grace, all were used together to explain the action of God in the world and in man, often in an allegorical way. These writers and the other teachers of the time were also very familiar with the Latin poets and prose writers, on whose works they produced careful and detailed commentaries, especially from a doctrinal standpoint. Here we touch on a characteristic difference between the Middle Ages and the sixteenth-century Renaissance: for the latter, what was important was literary style; for the former, the depth of the thought. Surely this is the eternal opposition of two kinds of learning and education: that of Plato and that of Isocrates.

Besides the making of such broad syntheses, the scholars of the twelfth century were also concerned with matters of narrower interest. They were keenly interested in the problems of psychology; this concern was common to the scholars and to the mystics, who were trying to clarify their experiences. Logic was also beginning to assert its claims; the whole of

Aristotle's *Organon* was now being used and a method of inquiry based primarily on deduction was being more and more clearly outlined. From this time on men lost all moderation in giving themselves up to the joys of dialectical argument: John of Salisbury mentions some of his fellow-students who studied logic in the school of Sainte Geneviève for twelve years. This logic was applied to all sorts of problems: ethical, psychological, metaphysical; and also theological. No longer was it enough to give a commentary on the Scriptures or the Fathers: given certain statements of revelation, their meaning was to be brought out by purely rational argument. St Anselm had made some efforts in this direction, but it was Abelard who first applied this method on a large scale, with all the power of his intellect, but also with that lack of restraint so typical of him. He began with the notion that the authorities in matters of doctrine contradict one another: some say, Yes, others, No (*sic et non*), so it rests with a man's reason to find the truth by personal reflection and by making careful distinctions.

This new theology immediately captured the schools and many masters were led to add systematic explanation to their exegesis. But this did not come about without causing a serious strain, which found its most dramatic expression in the dispute between Abelard and St Bernard. For, over and above the precise questions in which Abelard overstepped the bounds of orthodoxy, the fundamental attitude to theology, the direction of thought, of the two men was different. St Bernard—according to his professional colleague Otto of Freising—hated the dialecticians: he would have liked theology to remain a matter of personal meditation, of preaching, a matter of piety nurtured solely on the Scriptures and the Fathers, owing nothing to the reason, much less to systematic philosophy. The abbot of Clairvaux was well aware of the peculiar nature of monastic theology. But it is perhaps a pity that he refused to admit the possibility of another kind of theological inquiry, and that, albeit unwittingly, he laid the foundations of that opposition between scholastic and mystical theology which was later to deepen and widen still further.

The thirteenth century: the Scholastic or Aristotelian period

"Scholastic" must here be taken in its medieval sense. When Geoffrey of St Victor wanted to set aside a too technical question in his allegorical commentary on the Scriptures, he said he was leaving it to the "scholastic disputations", by which he clearly meant the courses, discussions and meetings arranged and run by the *scholastici*, that is, by the teachers. And it was in fact in the schools, and especially in the universities, that learning was professionally imparted. The city schools lost their importance, for the best masters and scholars gathered in a few centres, of which for the whole of the thirteenth century Paris was to be the most important. The schools of Paris won considerable autonomy in relation to the chancellor of the bishop of Paris; and the secular masters were there joined by the Dominicans, Franciscans and Carmelites. To all of these together a royal charter gave a status equivalent to that of the guilds, with masters (professors, doctors), journeymen (bachelors, assistant teachers), and apprentices (students). These were split into various faculties, not including law: there was no faculty of law in Paris, where it was thought that it would be too tempting to clerics, for whom the law was a gateway to lucrative employment. The Faculty of Arts was the most popular: it covered roughly the ground of our grammar school and the Arts Faculty of a modern university. The students were divided into different nations.

In all the faculties, the problem of the century was Aristotelianism. True, the principal courses of the Faculty of Theology were always devoted to the Scriptures. True also, there were always those who supported Platonism or Augustinianism. But Aristotelianism, with its clear logic and its systematic account of the world, everywhere made conquests. At the beginning of the century, it was thought possible to close the door firmly against it: the Church continued to banish it as in the patristic period. Then, about 1230, it seemed that a watered-down Aristotelianism might be admitted: a commission, even, was set up to expurgate the errors of the Stagirite. By 1245 it was obviously necessary to give in. Roger

Bacon was commenting on the *Physics*; and soon the powerful intellects of St Albertus Magnus and St Thomas Aquinas were to set forth their own interpretation which, taking up Aristotle's philosophy from within, at once improved it and gave it a new meaning. Within that system, which knew nothing of God's creation of the world, was developed that distinction between essence and existence which is the most perfect metaphysical expression of contingency. The meaning and importance of personality was affirmed in psychology, in ethics and in politics. It took the place of a system based on the ideas of species and collectivity.

It would have been too much to expect that this should achieve immediate success. A prophet is without honour in his own country; no man is a genius to his contemporaries. St Thomas was to remain always suspect to the supporters of traditional Augustinianism. He was even more threatened if not actually discredited by the excesses of men like Siger of Brabant. Siger was not a theologian, but was a member of the Faculty of Arts, and there taught a radical Aristotelianism tainted with Averroism. He adopted, in fact, certain ideas of Averroes, an Arabic philosopher of the twelfth century, who had given a strongly anti-religious flavour to the system.

The last years of the century were filled with the efforts of the Thomist and the Franciscan schools to discover exactly what was the place of Aristotle in philosophy and in theology.

The period of Nominalism

This is the last period of medieval philosophy. It is the least studied, and has been perhaps excessively criticized or praised according to the doctrinal prejudices of its judges. It is, however, beyond doubt that it failed to continue the great work of the thirteenth century, and its scepticism clearly marks a decline. Ockham had no faith in reason's power to support theology. For him, God was the Creator, and an arbitrary Master, whose designs and commands it was futile to try to understand. Moreover, there are no more general rules than there are abstract general ideas: everything is strictly an *individuum*, a separate individual, and every true act of knowledge is intuitive and is linked to one fact. In ethics, there are no virtues, there is only a discontinuous series of actions. It is obvious that nominalism denies the truth of any philosophy of general ideas or concepts, and of any theology of a God who takes reason to himself and gives it its highest expression. The natural sciences and politics were directed towards contingent ends and estimated in the same way in a similar context of ideas, with the result that both were able to profit by this to set themselves free, the first from natural philosophy and the second from a normative theory of ethics. But philosophy, like theology, was in for a rude shock: more than ever, Christendom was losing its consecrated character under the advancing influence of the secular, and the Renaissance was to draw all the consequences of this. The crowning point is that Ockham and his followers did not even put an end to the interminable discussion of all the old problems. They said again and again that the reason cannot establish certain knowledge but merely probabilities. These were enough, they thought, to justify their practising as professional theologians. Gabriel Biel says as much: it would be unworthy of a theologian or of a philosopher not to want to bring reason to bear on everything. Can we be surprised that these disciplines, in which their very teachers had ceased to believe, produced an uneasy feeling of dissatisfaction? The sixteenth century was to turn its back contemptuously on these logic-choppers, and to go back—with neither caution nor prudence, alas!—to the Classics and the Bible. But long before this, men of religious and mystical minds had left theology and philosophy as vain occupations and a temptation to pride. Nominalism brought medieval philosophy, and especially Scholasticism, into disrepute. So the distaste produced by the empty logic-chopping of nominalism has discredited also the realism of St Thomas, the exemplarism of St Bonaventure, and the Classicism or the Platonism of the twelfth century.

CHAPTER I

THE FOUNDERS OF THE MIDDLE AGES

BOËTHIUS

Boëthius, Cassiodorus, Isidore, Bede: these are the founders of medieval thought, those who provided it with its first literary expression and set it on the road it was to follow. The first, Boëthius, was a rich Roman of senatorial family who served the first barbarian kings of Italy at the same time as he did credit to his advanced philosophical education, acquired in the schools of Rome and Alexandria.

Boëthius' literary work, representing a considerable output, was produced with a very clear purpose: to provide for coming generations, whose education was threatened and who, in particular, knew no Greek, a series of essential textbooks. In this concern for education and the importance given to the schools Boëthius is already typically medieval. At that time, indeed, the literate public scarcely survived: it was almost exclusively to scholars and their pupils that intellectuals had to address themselves if they wanted an audience.

So, after producing in Latin, from Greek sources, textbooks of arithmetic and geometry, Boëthius decided to translate and comment on the works of Plato and Aristotle. Had it been completed, this grandiose scheme would have changed the intellectual history of the west, for at a single stroke all those books would have been inherited which only became known—and despite what difficulties!—in the thirteenth and fourteenth centuries. But Boëthius was unable to finish his work; he could get no further than the first part of Aristotle's logic, that which medieval scholars were to call the *logica vetus*. To this were added a few short treatises such as the translation of Porphyry's *Isagoge*, and textbooks of Boëthius' own, especially on the syllogism. The later Middle Ages was to go to these works for its formal logic and especially for the beginnings of the famous controversy over universals. For in commenting on a sentence in Porphyry Boëthius had raised the question of whether the ideas of genera and species which express the nature of things (man, horse, table, etc.) exist in reality or are only products of our reason. He takes no definite stand on this question but inclines to think that fundamentally these species are nothing other than concepts formed in the mind from the resemblances which unite individuals in such specific groups. Neither genus nor species is a reality in itself apart from things; it exists separately only in the human mind and in the divine Ideas. This is the solution of the modern realists, inspired partly by Aristotle and partly by Plato; both the "nominalists" and the "realists" exaggerated those elements congenial to their own attitude, in increasing the importance attached to *voces* (words) or *res* (things: that is, genera and species existing separately at least as divine Ideas).

Boëthius had as much influence in the religious field, for he wrote five short treatises, the *opuscula sacra*, on the problems of Trinitarian theology and Christology, which were being discussed by the intellectuals of his time. He clearly recognized that he was not a professional theologian, nor had he any technical education in exegesis or patrology. But his faith, which was deep and sincere, was scandalized by the differences which had shown themselves. As a logician and a metaphysician he wanted to intervene by the way of reason (*via rationis*) to clarify these questions by applying systematically to the Christian mysteries the concepts of relation, nature and person. Up to his time, theologians had used these words as parts of the ordinary vocabulary of everyday life. For Boëthius it was first and foremost important to establish a precise technical vocabulary, and then to apply it to dogma. This is clearly exactly what the theologians of the twelfth and thirteenth centuries did, and they, moreover, had a great regard for these writings of Boëthius.

Besides this, in one of these *opuscula*, the *De Hebdomadibus* (which was the title under which the Middle Ages knew the *Quomodo substantiae bonae sint*), Boëthius developed a metaphysics of participation, and adumbrated that distinction between essence and existence which was to be at the core of the Thomist metaphysics. Boëthius was in fact asking how beings can be intrinsically good while they are not the essential Good. His reply was that one must begin with the identification of Being and the Good. Everything exists because it participates in a first Being, which is God. In the same way everything is good because it receives its goodness from God. So there is a joint affirmation of both creation by God and the metaphysical value of beings thus brought into existence. What is more, the very structure of the created thing carries within it the mark of this participation: it is not its own being, but receives it through the mediation of its form. In each concrete being, the subject taken in its singular existence, comprising its matter and accidents, is something other than the form, which gives being; in God, on the other hand, they are one and the same.

Much more, however, than the logical or scholastic works of Boëthius, the Middle Ages loved, commented on and translated into the new vernaculars, Romance or Germanic, the *De Consolatione Philosophiae*. This work was written about the year 523, when the patrician Roman, in disgrace with the king and accused of treason, awaited his execution. In the tower that was his prison, the philosopher wrote this work to bring moral comfort and at the same time to give himself the chance to set out in one book the ideas he held dear. The book belongs both to the dialogue tradition and to that of the protreptic writings of Aristotle and Cicero (*Hortensius*). Boëthius describes himself as overwhelmed by misfortune; a woman appears to him in majesty—Philosophy herself. She has come to restore his courage and powers by making truth shine out before his eyes. She has no difficulty in diagnosing the nature of Boëthius' sickness: in the tumult of events and feelings he has lost sight of the true end of man.

All things are ruled by God. It is in himself, by turning back into himself, that man learns his origin and destiny (Book 1). True happiness cannot consist in the possession of the uncertain goods provided by fortune, but must be sought within: the intellectual and moral value of the immortal soul. All external goods, riches, honours, power, or glory, are unreal, sham and merely external. The true wise man does not strive after them, and knows well, when he does possess them, that their only value is derived from the way he as a man, as a moral being, uses them (Book 2). Obviously, Boëthius is here speaking in the direct tradition from Socrates and the Stoics: truth and virtue are the only real goods, the only riches no man can take away. He thus acts as a link between the ethical systems of antiquity and the Middle Ages. All those, as does the *Consolatio*, prefix their actual teaching by a consideration of the nature of the real and true Good and a criticism of secondary values. But Boëthius, more perhaps than others, has the merit of having shown that this supreme Good must be sought and found by each man in himself. Thereby he began the medieval tradition Etienne Gilson happily called "Christian Socratism". Book 3 goes on to deepen this same idea: the aim is to lead the reader not only to seek truth and virtue in himself but him who is their origin and end: that is, God. At the same time, the temptation of purely human happiness is considered in its manifestations—riches, honours, power, glory, pleasure. What man mistakenly seeks in these imperfect goods can only be found in its fullness in God. He is at once perfect Being and the sovereign Good. To gain God, to become oneself divine, to be God by participation, this is to be happy. In speaking in this way, be it noticed, Boëthius is in the tradition of the ancient ethics, but he distinguishes more carefully than his authorities the objective Good which is God, the participation of man in this Good, and the happiness he derives from this participation. The profound inspiration of the first pages of the *Secunda pars* of St Thomas is the same. Both authors really wish to say that the desire for happiness, on the psychological level, and the orientation towards the Good, on the ontological level, are directly rooted in the nature of man, and are part of the irreducible minimum of self-love which no man can or ought to do without.

It remains to reconcile the theory set out with the facts of life. The righteous man is happy even in adversity. Yet he does suffer, despite his participation in God, while the wicked can enjoy the good things of this life. How ought we to understand the government of God? How do we reconcile the existence of a good God with the existence of evil? Philosophy's answer to Boëthius is that the wicked have no true power or happiness. The reward of every action lies in itself, as vice punishes itself by its very existence. Moreover, unhappiness is of use to men (Book 4). All the same, we want to understand how God governs the world, and how his providence allows for man's freedom. The problem Boëthius is posing is not that of the scholastics who sought to reconcile freewill and that working of grace necessary for man to do good. Nor is he concerned, as the ancients had been, with defining the exact rôle of fate. More than that, Boëthius is careful to keep spiritual beings like men outside the field of operation of fate. Obviously for him the human person is much too noble to be tossed about by the blind interplay of events: it depends on a personal Providence. It is precisely concerning God's providence and the knowledge he has of events that the problem is formulated: how can God's knowledge of future events be necessarily certain when they depend on man's free will? Boëthius is aware that he is tackling this question in a new way in considering the mode of knowing proper to God. He is not in time, past, present and future, but in eternity; so he sees free decisions not as future but as present. From his eternal present God sees things as they will be, that is, as free. The necessity belongs to the character of the knowledge, not the fact known.

Thus Boëthius has left in the *Consolatio* a great philosophical work, including a metaphysics of participation, a study of God, and a system of ethics. Some astonishment has been expressed that he did not make the work more explicitly Christian. But only a moderate surprise should be felt. Boëthius was a thinker who, like many other Christians of antiquity, had received two distinct educations, so to speak: one exclusively Platonic, the other Christian. He played well on both instruments, a master in logic as in Christology. But when he needed to synthesize the two systems of thought he met with many difficulties. Certainly he often gives a Christian meaning to pagan ideas he uses, and certainly his Christianity is always there as a back-cloth. Nonetheless, all the concords are not complete, nor are all the necessary extensions of thought achieved. Boëthius would perhaps be better understood if some contemporary Christians were borne in mind. They are those whose Christianity is derived entirely from within the family, but whose university education has been exclusively secular. Beyond doubt some reconciling of the two systems of thought is achieved, yet—at least such is the impression one frequently gets—the two categories of thought often remain independent.

Are we not also too severe and too suspicious? Compare the ethics of Boëthius with that of the *Secunda pars* of St Thomas, the inspiration of which, as we have just remarked, is the same. No one would deny St Thomas the qualities of the theologian, the saint and the mystic; and yet the ethics of the *Summa* seems more philosophical than theological, there is more talk of God than of Christ, and, in any instance, the concrete forms of the Gospel ethics are not as often recalled as in the commentaries on the Scriptures. Again, St Thomas did not scruple to put his ethics in the second part of his *Summa* and Christ in the third. Why? Because when he wrote his ethics, the great doctor wanted above all to present a synthesis the models for which were, in the works of the philosophers and especially of Aristotle, more exact than in the occasional and episodic teaching of the Scriptures. Like Boëthius, he obeyed the rules for the kind of work he was writing and the influence of a literary inspiration directly governed by the sources he was using. Because he showed himself to be a philosopher, Boëthius was not less of a Christian—a Christian philosopher; which demonstrates the truth of what was said earlier, that this Christian philosophy preserved a real autonomy and a real integrity.

CASSIODORUS

Cassiodorus was born a few years later than Boëthius, about 485, at Squillace in southern Italy, an estate his family, of Syrian origin, had acquired in the service of the last Roman emperors. He received an almost exclusively Latin education—with a core, that is, of grammar, rhetoric and law—and while still very young entered the service of the barbarian kings. He was still scarcely twenty when he became official assistant to his father, the praetorian prefect. He then climbed the ladder of office from quaestor to consul and finally *magister officiorum*, a kind of secretary of state. That Cassiodorus escaped the fate of Boëthius and Pope John II was due to his essential opportunism. More than once in his historical works he flatters the Goths outrageously. He suffered only minor troubles and dishonour: he was simply banished from the royal court and given tasks outside Rome. His return to favour brought him the title of "patrician".

Paradoxically, it was the Byzantine reconquest of Italy that finally banished him from public life. Even then he was able to ingratiate himself and stay for a time in Constantinople, but never again did he take an active part in public affairs. After the fashion of retired politicians, he published the documents and letters of his time of office, the *Variae*, to which later medieval chancelleries often went for models to copy.

Ever since his first troubles, Cassiodorus had entered on a process of both religious and intellectual development. Not only did his spiritual life deepen but he took up the defence of the ever more threatened ancient culture. This was one of his chief characteristics: it is shown in the production of works on the soul or on the Psalms, but still more in the foundation of a "Catholic university" in Rome, with the approval of Pope Agapitus (535–6). The wars between the Goths and the

Byzantines did not allow this venture to survive for long; in particular, Cassiodorus' fine library was scattered. But he took up the idea again on new lines when he founded on his land in south Italy, in 555, the monastery of Vivarium (so called because of the fishponds which surrounded it). Cassiodorus himself was probably never a monk, but he certainly had considerable influence over the community, which was governed by monastic principles close to those of St Benedict, those of the *Regula Magistri*, of which Cassiodorus may well have been the author. The monastery was no less severe in respect to the religious life than others of the age, but the presence and influence of Cassiodorus gave it a quite peculiar intellectual bias which contrasts with the strictness of the first Benedictine monasteries.

It was for his monks that Cassiodorus wrote his *De Institutione*, which was to be the first treatise of monastic studies as well as the first *ratio studiorum* for the education of the medieval clergy. As late as the twelfth century, Hugh of St Victor sticks closely to it in drawing up his programme of study. We can safely say that it was not finally forgotten and left behind until the thirteenth century.

The work, written about 560, consists of two books which often exist independently in the manuscript tradition, for the first was less often copied than the second. This deals with the study of theology, and there monks and clerics felt able to stand on their own feet. Cassiodorus first provides introductions to the books of the Scriptures, setting out the essential ideas of their authors, the kind of book each is, and its teaching. Then he goes on to the tradition and the teaching which should guide the Christian in his study of the Scriptures. And finally, he gives some information about the great Latin commentators, Hilary, Cyprian, Ambrose, Jerome and Augustine. According to our modern systematization, we should say that he was dealing with positive theology, but, for his age, this was all theology, for the few "scholastic" treatises of Boëthius and Isidore found no successors until the twelfth century.

Much more noticed by the Middle Ages—and much more

worthy of notice by the historian of Christian philosophy—was
the second part of the *De Institutione*, devoted to secular learning; it was in fact a condensation of all the Roman experience
in education.

The work is really a kind of introduction to the seven
liberal arts: the *trivium*, grammar, rhetoric, dialectic, and the
quadrivium, arithmetic, geometry, astronomy and music. For
each of these disciplines, Cassiodorus gives definitions and the
basic ideas and rules, and at the same time quotes the writers
to whom reference should be made for more complete study.
Like Martianus Capella's *Marriage of Mercury and Philology*,
this second book of the *De Institutione* was to be a classic for
secular studies, and to assure some knowledge, if elementary,
in fields otherwise completely closed to the medieval student
and scholar. Its author declares, indeed, that this knowledge is
absolutely necessary to anyone who wishes to study the
Scriptures with profit or advance in theology.

At first sight it may look as though philosophy is excluded
from this cycle of studies. Happily this is not so; the treatise
on dialectic, fuller than the others, provides more than its title
would lead one to believe. Philosophy is included under that
Christian guise spoken of in the Introduction, for it is defined
as the knowledge of things human and divine, as the discipline
of disciplines, the queen of the sciences, a meditation on death,
and assimilation to God. These are so many phrases reminis-
cent of Platonism, to which Cassiodorus clearly gave a Christian
meaning. But as we said above, the assimilation of this philosophical inquiry to theology is not complete, for theology is
founded on the Scriptures (Book 1 of the *De Institutione*),
while philosophy was taught by the pagans: a distinction entirely practical and hardly very profound, but none the less
significant.

This philosophy is presented by Cassiodorus in the schematic
form with all its divisions as it had been established by the
Platonic Aristotelian syncretism, the technical terms of which
were taken from Ammonius. First there is speculative philosophy, which studies things in themselves and is subdivided

according to the three degrees of abstraction. Natural philosophy (which was also called "physics" and which nowadays would also be called cosmology) has as its object the external world, things as subject to change. The second degree of abstraction is that of the sciences of the *quadrivium*, forming theoretical philosophy, that of abstract quantity. Lastly, divine philosophy studies things separate from matter, God and spiritual creatures. Beside the speculative philosophy there is practical philosophy, divided into logic, the tool or instrument of correct thinking, and moral philosophy, the rule of correct living. Moral philosophy is subdivided into ethics proper, economics and politics. This is an incomplete account of the matter but it was enough to make reasonably justifiable within the traditional forms a revival of rational ethics from the twelfth century onwards; that is, before the ethical works of Aristotle became known.

The lion's share is given by Cassiodorus to logic. This is normal practice during the first part, and almost during the whole, of the Middle Ages. For in the universities' Arts faculties in the fourteenth and fifteenth centuries logic had two years of study devoted to it for the one left to the other divisions of philosophy. The medieval scholars had a feeling for dialectic and seemed to enjoy it above all else. It is true that this logic included many philosophical concepts. This is easily seen in this second book of the *De Institutione* where, in summarizing Aristotle's logic, Cassiodorus explains what the ten metaphysical categories are and takes the opportunity of defining first and second substances, quantity, quality and temporality (*quando*).

But the historian of medieval thought is more interested in the *De Anima* than in these elementary textbooks, the importance of which is historical rather than doctrinal. The *De Anima* was written just when Cassiodorus was leaving public life and beginning his religious retreat. It is strictly traditional in its dialogue form, its method, which mixes together questions of psychology and those of ethics, and the materials it uses.

Looking for a definition of the soul, Cassiodorus found himself faced with two traditions. On the one hand were the Stoics and the ancient doctors, who saw in the soul primarily a principle of life more or less the same as the matter it made living. On the other side were the Platonists and the Fathers, making of it a spiritual entity, rational, immaterial, transcending the material organism. Throughout the Middle Ages the opposition between these two conceptions of the soul continued, for we have to wait until St Thomas to reach a reconciliation of the idea of the subsistent soul with that of the soul as the form of the body. Cassiodorus, for his part, remains faithful to Christian Platonism and, at the risk of weakening his explanation of the union of soul and body, insists on the spirituality of the former. He rejects the insinuation of Stoic ideas into Christianity, and condemns any concession to materialism. In this he was opposing Tertullian and Faustus of Riez, who interpreted the parable of Dives and Lazarus over-literally in the tradition of psychological materialism.

But he is less categorical when he has to describe the activity of the soul. On the one hand we have the four cardinal virtues, and on the other the Platonic trinity of spirit, reason and memory. To this he adds a list of five "natural virtues", in which the will and pleasure rub shoulders with the *virtus vitalis*, the *sensus intelligentiae* and the *virtus principalis*. Here again Cassiodorus is a link between ancient and medieval. Like many later thinkers, he stays on a very practical level, partly because of lack of method, and partly because of respect for traditional classifications. His readers, such as those of the early Middle Ages, perhaps sought less to investigate the richness of the intellectual and ethical life than to find assistance in exegesis and definitions of traditional terms. A man like Alcher of Clairvaux says no more in the twelfth century, and satisfies the curiosity of his fellow-monks, who wanted above all to find in psychology a means of seeing things clearly in their spiritual life. But how inferior to Aristotle did these authors seem when the thirteenth century read his actual writings and discovered in him positive analyses of the soul's faculties and their interaction.

ISIDORE OF SEVILLE

Isidore came of a Romanized Spanish family which had fled from Cartagena when the Goths came and had established themselves in Seville. There, about 570, Isidore was born. The death of his father left him in the care of his elder brother Leander, who was to precede him as Archbishop of Seville. The names of the two brothers, and those of the other two children also, Fulgentius and Florentinus, have been inscribed in the roll of the martyrs.

Leander was himself educated, and had Isidore educated also, in a specifically Christian atmosphere, in particular at the episcopal school of Seville. It may be that Isidore was entrusted to the care of a monastery while Leander went on an embassy to Constantinople. He went to seek the aid of the *Basileus* for Hermengild, the Catholic Visigothic prince, against the Arian kings, just as St Gregory, whom he met and stayed with, was asking in the name of the pope the assistance of the Byzantines against the Lombards. Isidore's remarkable education shows clearly the vitality of the ecclesiastical schools of the early Middle Ages. The public schools of the Roman period had by then practically disappeared from Spain. Clerics and monks took over from them and taught their pupils, future clerks themselves, secular and divine literature together.

Isidore, as was natural, helped his brother in his episcopal ministry and his apostolate—which culminated in the conversion of the Visigothic king Reccared to Catholicism in 589 —and he succeeded him in the see of Seville in 601, which he graced for thirty-five years until his death on April 4th, 636. He played an eminent part both in religion and politics in Spain, helping to re-shape the Church and civil society there. It can be truly said that he stands precisely at the point where the Romano-Spanish society, which was disappearing, joins the new Spain of the Visigoths: his life marks exactly the transition from antiquity to the Middle Ages.

There are in the huge corpus of Isidore's works two to which the historian of medieval Christian philosophy must give particular consideration: the *Etymologiae sive Origines* and the *Sententiae*. The first is an immense encyclopedia in which was gathered the sum of the ancient knowledge: the Middle Ages were to go to it as an almost universal source-book. It deals with: grammar, rhetoric, dialectic, arithmetic, geometry, music, astronomy, medicine, law and ethics, chronography, the Bible, theology, the Church and its organization, pagan philosophy, psychology, animals, cosmography, mineralogy, agriculture, the art of war, the theatre, navigation, architecture, textile manufacture, cookery and travel. The second work, the *Sententiae*, is a systematic *summa* fundamentally concerned with faith and morals; it draws its conclusions from the patristic writings and in its method foreshadows the theological syntheses of the twelfth century.

Isidore is one of those medieval writers who can never be made to fit our modern categories of philosopher or theologian. He is the very type of Christian philosopher when he defines philosophy (*Etym.* II, 24) and wisdom (*Sent.* II, 1) as the knowledge of things human and divine. It is in this knowledge that the nature of man is truly fulfilled (the *vita beata* of the Greek and Latin philosophers) by the conquest of truth and virtue. To reach this goal, the study of the ancients is useful, but much more is that of revelation. It is in revelation, and in the sacred Scriptures themselves, as in Genesis, Ecclesiastes, Proverbs, the Song of Songs, and the Gospel, that physics, ethics and logic are to be found (*Etym.* II, 24). The most thoroughgoing harmony was thus initiated, and the Archbishop of Seville was setting forth the idea of one united corpus of knowledge. Christian principles were joined in it with philosophical elements drawn from the Neo-Platonist tradition.

In his metaphysics Isidore begins with God as the source of all good and all incorruptibility. Angels and men are only good by participation and in a limited way. Matter introduces in them potentiality, which checks the dynamic power of the form. Beauty, unity and greatness are fully realized only in God, but they exist in man and other creatures as "vestiges": there are thus degrees in being as in the knowledge one can have of it.

Isidore here freely welds the Christian idea of the image of God in man to that of Platonic participation. He uses it in the same way in dealing with the problem of evil, the existence of which, on the ontological level, he denies. Everything is by its nature necessarily good in so far as it exists. If there is evil on the moral level, it is because man has introduced it there. On the level of the physical world, because of and following the fall of man, natural forces are no longer perfectly coordinated (*Sent.* I, 1–9).

Man is made of a body and a soul in somewhat painful union, since the soul loses much of its glory in being incarcerated in the flesh (*Sent.* I, 12). The action of the senses—described with a great wealth of detail in *Etym.* XI—is a compromise of flesh and spirit. This makes possible the higher psychological activity which forms images in the memory, and then thought comes in, with the will, and gives the soul a life worthy of itself. Because of its imprisonment in the flesh the soul's knowledge of itself is defective. Yet it is full of richness and power: Isidore goes over its qualities following St Augustine, glossing each of the names of the spirit: image of God, memory, animating principle of the body, will, thought, reason, sense.

This is all only a commonplace Neo-Platonism, which was all Christians had until the triumph of Aristotelianism. Yet against this, Isidore was more original, and had more influence on the history of western thought, in his teaching in the realm of morals and politics. He it was who handed on to the Middle Ages the teaching of the Roman jurists on the natural law. He defined it as the moral and juridical expression of the demands of our nature, at once sensible and spiritual. Before any positive statement of civil law or international law (*ius gentium*, that is, the laws common to all nations), the natural law ruled the sexual and social life of men. On it rested a fundamental demand for the liberty and dignity of each individual (*Etym.* V). In one sense, Isidore also belongs to the Aristotelian tradition, which drew an essential distinction between natural and statute law. According to the Nicomachean Ethics (V, 7), the first is based on nature itself, everywhere of the same authority, independent of shifts of opinion. On the other hand, what belongs to statute or positive law is not so determined by nature, before the expressed requirements of the legislator; its object was capable of being determined in various ways.

A very great service was thus rendered by Isidore to ethics. He showed that law is above all the expression of a natural need or will, belonging to the moral nature of man. It is not a more or less arbitrary, external command. Still less does it depend on the tyrannical will of this or that king or governor. In those barbarian times it was a timely truth to recall.

Isidore was equally concerned to recall to the great and powerful, especially to kings and governors, the duties of their office. He granted them the widest powers only as instruments in God's hand, for the triumph of the good and the protection of the weak. Indeed, for Isidore the king's was a vocation, a mission. His title *rex* came from *recte agere*, and implied that the king should act rightly himself and see that his subjects did also. Isidore was not afraid to see kings wielding some power in the Church, for their authority worked for ecclesiastical discipline. What the priest could not achieve by persuasion the king obtained through fear. So the kingdom of God profited from the kingdom of this world, and the latter received its duties and powers from the former (*Sent.* III, 51). If God wished some men to be raised to such high dignity despite the fundamental equality of human kind, it was in order that they might do good, and particularly that they might protect Christians. To this moral vocation corresponded an absolute power: no one subordinate to the king might oppose him except the bishops, the interpreters of what was right. We seem here to be stepping into a wholly medieval theocracy.

THE VENERABLE BEDE

Bede must be mentioned here not only for his intellectual genius but also as representing the Anglo-Saxon centres of learning. In this first period of the Middle Ages it was, as we can see, the peninsular or insular parts of Europe that led the way. Until the Franks re-entered the picture with the Carolingian renaissance other countries preserved and spread the love of learning and wisdom.

Augustine, the monk sent by St Gregory to England, had organized monastic and cathedral schools, and two generations later Rome appointed as Archbishop of Canterbury a Greek monk, Theodore, who was eager to spread his language and his culture. One of his pupils, Benedict Biscop, founded two monasteries in Northumberland, at Wearmouth and Jarrow. These he set up as Benedictine houses and endowed them, particularly Jarrow, with precious books brought back from Italy. Some scholars consider that some of these books came from Vivarium; in any case, it is important that something of the spirit of Cassiodorus was planted in England. English monks throughout the Middle Ages had a strong tendency towards both direct missionary works and intellectual activity. Perhaps this can be put down to the practical character of the Anglo-Saxon peoples, but the missionary character of the society from which they came may also have counted for something. At any rate schools and teaching were for these monks and preachers an indispensable means of influence and a necessary condition of progress.

It was in the monastery at Jarrow that Bede, born in 673 on the monastery estates, was educated and then himself taught. His influence in learned circles spread rapidly, especially to the neighbouring cathedral school at York. His writings included, besides the justly famous *Ecclesiastical History of the English Nation*, works on grammar, exegesis, hagiography, philosophy and the sciences of the *quadrivium*, all of which were frequently to be used as textbooks in the medieval schools.

CHAPTER II

THE CAROLINGIAN RENAISSANCE

SCHOOLS AND MOVEMENTS

When Charlemagne restored the western Roman Empire on the political level, he thought it proper to continue the ancient tradition in the cultural sphere also. Besides, he had been chosen by the Church to succeed Byzantium, whose influence was waning; so he felt he ought to play the same part, in the development of the Church's institutions and doctrine, as the emperors had played earlier in the great councils, and as Isidore explicitly allowed to the Christian monarch. This supposed that the king would have around him and throughout the empire an educated official class and an educated clergy. Charlemagne regarded himself as the heir of the great kings of Israel, charged in this latter day with the task of bringing the people of God into the ways of the Lord so as to establish and exalt his Law.

These are some of the ideas developed in the *capitula* in which the emperor ordered that schools be opened in all cathedrals and monasteries. He himself set the example in opening a school in the court which was to be a sort of nursery for future civil, military and religious officials, and in surrounding himself with a group of cultivated minds—or minds at least wanting to appear cultivated. This group was normally known as the Palatine Academy, because of the constant references its members made to the garden in Athens where Plato taught.

The emperor was followed with varying degrees of willingness.

Flourishing episcopal schools were opened at Metz and Lyons, but it was particularly the great monasteries which were to be most influential in this movement, both as regards the actual teaching and as regards the diffusion of manuscripts. The importance of their work, on both Christian and pagan texts, which allowed the west to renew its contact with the past and western thought to profit from the total achievement of the ancient traditions, cannot be overestimated.

But the best projects are only valuable in proportion to the quality of the men who put them into practice. So Charlemagne was equally concerned to keep by him on his travels, or to encourage to come together in his empire, the best elements from the centres of learning which still existed. From Lombard Italy came Peter of Pisa, a grammarian, Paulinus of Aquileia, and, soon after, Paul the Deacon. From Spain came Leidrad and then Agobard, both future bishops of Lyons, and Theodulph, who was to occupy the see of Orleans. But it was from England and Ireland that the most active and original minds were to come. At their head was Alcuin, taught by pupils of Bede at York, future Abbot of Tours, and the counsellor who chiefly had the ear of the emperor. The renaissance of learning was in large measure his work. He formulated the principles which were to guide it and educated men to spread the same ideas far and wide, especially in Germany, at Fulda, where Rhabanus Maurus taught, *praeceptor Germaniae*.

For some time before the Irish had been coming across the Channel, for travel abroad, *peregrinatio*, for Christ's sake was for them an essential element of their devotion. They brought with them an original cast of mind in which were mixed, together with mysticism, a great curiosity for all branches of learning and a very characteristic preciosity of language. Their contemporaries always referred to this extraordinary language, abounding in Greek forms and the oddest neologisms, as *pultes Scottica*, "Scots' (i.e. Irish) porridge". These Irish scholars had an enormous influence on the development of thought, so much so as to arouse constant jealousy and suspicion; and they gave to the Carolingian renaissance the only philosopher who really spread his wings, that John who by long custom is called by an odd tautology Scotus Erigena.

In what spirit did these teachers and their pupils work? What they wanted, fundamentally, was to make themselves the mouthpieces of "wisdom", of *philosophia* in the broadest sense of the word, as it is expressed in the Christian message. Their studies had a religious aim: they were intended to form clerics as well as educated laymen who should assist the Church in her work. In that way, Christian doctrine would be defended and Christian people instructed.

With this end in mind, the writers of the ninth century went to the Fathers, for whom they had the greatest admiration. This was not, as in the twelfth century, a matter of climbing on the shoulders of giants so as to see further than they (John of Salisbury, *Metalogicon*, III, 55, quoting Bernard of Chartres). The men of the ninth century stayed at the feet of the Fathers and listened reverently to the oracles proceeding from their lips. When a problem arose, the first thing to do was draw up a list of patristic quotations and sum up the traditional teaching. The declarations of the Council of Frankfurt in 794 are quite explicit: "Why should not statements contained in the writings of the Fathers and confirmed by the tradition of the Church be sufficient for us? The Scripture says that we should not go beyond the limits set by our fathers. Are we wiser than they?"

So it was, in principle, for the better understanding of the Scriptures and the Fathers that the liberal arts and the classical authors were studied. Did not the ancient Christian writers tell us, as others have, that the study of dialectic is necessary both to refute heresies and to penetrate more deeply the meaning of the Scriptures? Let no one then presume to want to reason beyond what is given to us in the faith; or worse, to argue against it in the name of dialectic. In this, the ninth century fell far short of the twelfth, and by its suspicious attitude of mind made the development of "scholasticism", of a dialectical theology, and still more the development of an autonomous philosophy, impossible.

Yet renewed contact with pagan texts ended by making people think in a less exclusively religious way, and by stirring up problems more philosophical than theological. Psychology and logic raise problems of their own which cannot be evaded simply because they have been met with in Virgil, Ovid, Cicero, Boëthius, or Martianus Capella. Man is made in the likeness of God; true, but he has also a nature which can be defined on its own. What relations should we posit between man's soul and his body? What sort of actions are thinking and willing? And, especially, what is the true meaning and worth of the general, generic concepts we constantly use?

Such are some of the philosophical problems raised within this theocratic world of thought of this period. They are raised in independent works (*opuscula*) as well as in commentaries on Genesis or glosses on the ancient grammarians.

THE BEGINNINGS

Alcuin holds first place among those who began the Carolingian renaissance. Attached to the royal court, he had such great influence on Charlemagne that all the emperor's measures bear the easily recognizable mark, down to the actual words used in their formulation, of his counsellor. But the written work of this Anglo-Saxon scholar is less important than his achievement in the field of education. Besides a few textbooks, he left a *De Trinitate*, occasioned by the Adoptionist controversy, and an inexhaustible store of arguments for controversialists; a *De rhetorica et virtutibus*; and a *De animæ ratione*. This last work, addressed to a cousin of Charlemagne, Eulalia (also called Gundrad), who had been interested in a debate on the subject at one of the meetings of the palace school, was very little like a textbook of psychology. It was rather an introduction to the Christian life which took as its starting point the idea of *order* which the soul must recognize in its situation between God on the one hand and lower creatures, especially the human body, on the other.

The soul possesses certain faculties, the same faculties

described by Plato and handed down to Alcuin by Cassian and Isidore of Seville: *rationalis, irascibilis, concupiscibilis*; and also certain virtues or powers which help to preserve spiritual harmony. Having been made in the likeness of God, the soul bears in itself the image of the Trinity in the intelligence, the memory and the will. This we can recognize as an Augustinian idea which enjoyed a considerable vogue throughout the Middle Ages and is here reduced to its simplest terms. Alcuin also reproduces the Augustinian theory of perception, but does not go into its metaphysical basis. As for the problem of the origin of the soul, Augustine had always refused to commit himself, and Alcuin followed the example of his caution.

The *De anima* which Rhabanus Maurus, a pupil of Alcuin's, sent to the young king of Germany, Lothair II, was still narrower in its scope. He was most concerned to remind the king of the practice of virtue and the importance of military valour. This explains why, after a few chapters borrowed from Cassiodorus and emptied of what little substance they had retained in that author, Rhabanus should take his time in studying through five chapters the virtues in general and the four cardinal virtues, for he was reproducing an extract from a work on military tactics itself borrowed from Vegetius. Here, then, under the pretence of dealing with psychology, our author "moralizes", in the worst sense of the word. Fortunately, Rhabanus wrote other works, in particular a vast *De universo*, which renewed contact, through Isidore, with the encyclopedic tradition of Pliny the Younger, and made free use of all fields of knowledge and all authorities. This freedom depended upon two notions frequently recurring in the Middle Ages: that of "spoiling the Egyptians", when the Israelites left Egypt, or the foreign women taken as wives by the Israelites; and that taken from Origen, that Christians should have no false shame in using pagan writers since they, far from being initiators, were imitators. Physics, ethics, logic, all first occur in the Bible; Christians, then, are only taking back from the pagans what never really belonged to them.

Without perhaps explicitly desiring it, Rhabanus Maurus

thus provided the basis for a culture existing for its own sake. His work, besides constituting a mine of information, rendered great service to the cause of philosophy and the development of philosophical ideas.

The only writer of this generation who seems really original is Benedict of Aniane, the reformer of the Benedictine order. Besides a *Concordia regularum*, we owe to him a work on the bases of faith which was read and plagiarized before being set in order again by a disciple of Rhabanus Maurus, the monk Candidus. The *Dicta Candidi*, which should thus really be attributed to Benedict of Aniane, sets out, among other things, the first dialectical proof for the existence of God the Middle Ages knew. Man, because of his knowledge, is set above lower creatures which simply exist or live, and so he acquires the idea of a hierarchical order and that of perfection. Knowing himself to be short of perfection, he therefore recognizes the existence of supreme perfection, which is God. Augustine's words are not here slavishly reproduced, but serve merely as the basis of personal reflection and elaboration of their substance. The same is true of the fragment on the image of the Trinity in the soul, which was copied at least eight times before the *De Spiritu et anima* of Alcher of Clairvaux.

If metaphysics and psychology seem therefore not to have spread their wings in the first years of the Carolingian renaissance, the same is not true of moral philosophy. We have already remarked how Alcuin and Rhabanus Maurus, when they wrote "on the soul" (*de anima*), used the occasion to write on the nature and the classification of the vices and the virtues. Two "mirrors of princes" were produced in the field of ethics for laymen: Jonas of Orleans' *De institutione regia* is useful as showing what clerics thought about the secular powers and the reciprocal relations between the spiritual and the temporal; and some years later an Irishman, Sedulius, wrote in his turn a *Liber de rectoribus*. Under the same heading we can mention Rhabanus Maurus' *De virtutibus et vitiis*, addressed to Louis the Fair, who was then in open conflict with his sons. And we could equally well include the *Liber Dodanae* (or *Duodenae*) *manualis*, in which a mother, the wife of Count Bernard of Septimania, exhorts her son William not to follow the paths of wickedness, which merely beget vexation and unrest. It is a sort of profit and loss account, and evidence of the level of thought and culture the best elements of Carolingian society could reach.

The most enigmatic figure in the first generation of Alcuin's disciples is surely Fredegis, Abbot of St Martin's at Tours and chancellor of Louis the Pious. Of his work only the *Epistola de nihilo et tenebris* survives, the meaning of which is still debated. Was he posing an exegetical problem concerning the creation of the world beginning from that chaos on which the darkness lay? Was he being metaphysical and hypostatizing a privative term?

Agobard of Lyons accused him also of believing in the pre-existence of the soul, since he used a somewhat ambiguous expression. The soul, said the archbishop, is created at the same time as the body it animates. This assertion, which he does not attempt to prove, nevertheless marks a step forward. Cassiodorus, Alcuin and Rhabanus Maurus had all remained undecided on this subject, following Augustine. The uncertainty continued to exist for a long time, as texts from various sources but all of about the same date, around 850, serve to show. On one side the Anglo-Saxon monk Gottschalk, well known because of his strict interpretation of the Augustinian doctrine of predestination, tried to establish a middle position between the creationism of St Jerome and the traducianism suggested but never fully adopted by St Augustine. For Gottschalk the souls of men are all derived from Adam's soul (and so the handing on of original sin would be explained), but their emergence as particular souls distinct from those of the parents needs the special intervention of God. This solution remained practically unknown, except to Hincmar of Rheims; we know from Flodoard that he touched on this problem in his treatise called *Ferculum Salomonis*. At almost the same time, in the Christian community of Toledo which survived in Moslem Spain, two laymen, Alvarez of Cordova and his brother-in-law John, exchanged letters in which the former, although he had amassed a good deal of evidence, felt bound to admit that questions concerning man's soul are often insoluble. John's reply is well known chiefly because it contains a long fragment of a work attributed to St Ambrose, which might be part of his lost *De philosophia*. It should be noticed that Alvarez refers to Claudianus Mamertus, but rejects the spiritist hypothesis in favour of the ideas of St Hilary, known for his materialist conception of the soul.

THE MID-CENTURY

All this indicates that the ideas of St Augustine, which had until this time been reckoned beyond questioning, were one by one again being disputed.

We can say without fear of contradiction that the best example of this process is the controversy concerning pre-destination. It belongs properly to the history of dogma, but it might have produced some new thinking on this crucial problem of the relations and the balance between the foreknowledge and will of God on the one hand, and man's freedom on the other. But in fact, the protagonists in this debate, Gottschalk and his later supporters, Prudentius of Troyes and Florus of Lyons, as much as their opponents, merely threw at the others' heads collections of texts culled from St Augustine in which his thought, already difficult to understand fully, was, like his authority, considerably undermined. But if the argument contributed nothing new on the basic problem of human destiny, it nevertheless caused many texts to be re-read, and it stirred up various related questions, one of which at least is now of interest to us.

In the court of Charles the Bald, where the argument had been followed with interest, a new debate arose, this time on the nature of the soul and its relation to the body. Two of the contributory causes seem to have been the reading of the arguments of the Augustinians and the semi-Pelagians of the fifth century, and the new questioning of Augustine's authority.

Hincmar of Rheims and Ratramnus of Corbie each received a list of questions drawn up by order of the king. He wanted them to express definite opinions on these points: is the soul corporeal, is it contained in the body and does it move with the body? Is every created thing corporeal and only God incorporeal? Can the soul escape from the limitation of the body? And so on; a whole series of questions as to the metaphysical status of created spirits, angels and souls, in their relations among themselves and to the body. Hincmar and Ratramnus set to work and each produced his chain of quotations, but not without giving first his personal opinions. Hincmar held that the soul was circumscribed by the limits of the body. Ratramnus insisted on its spiritual character, and invoked the Augustinian argument from the *De quantitate animae* in order to say that the soul was not in any place whatever. Logic was important in this debate, which raised yet again the problem of universals.

It was in the same controversy over predestination that there first appears an Irishman who, for a few centuries at least, provided matter for discussion: John Scotus Erigena. We know practically nothing about him before this date, 849–50, when he was asked by Hincmar to give his opinion on the points in dispute. He was already known and teaching at the palace school; there he commented on the *Marriage of Philology and Mercury* of Martianus Capella and the *Consolation of Philosophy* of Boëthius. Our account of this early teaching of Erigena is still far from complete, because the manuscript tradition through which we know it is not absolutely clear or reliable. But we can at least see him trying to discover the philosophic truths hidden under the myth which describes Philology taken up into the heavens to be the bride of Mercury. During her ascent and before she is enthroned among the gods, Philology has to undergo certain purificatory rites, is overwhelmed with gifts, and is finally admitted to sit among them. The names of the gods, the interpretation of the gifts, everything was matter for comment. Erigena based his commentary on a wide reading, in the forefront of which we can trace

Chalcidius' commentary on Plato's *Timaeus*, possibly Macrobius' commentary on the *Somnium Scipionis*, Servius' glosses on Virgil, the mythological writers, and Isidore of Seville, the *Encyclopaedia Britannica* of the age. There is therefore no need to be surprised if we meet with allusions to Neo-Platonic doctrines or the whole philosophical cosmology of late antiquity.

All this is very revealing of the way men's minds were changing in the middle of the ninth century. For Erigena was not unique, as is too often believed by those who think only of the second half of his life and work. Lupus of Ferrières was establishing critical texts of Cicero, and comparing the *Catilines* with the corresponding texts of Sallust. Hadoard, a somewhat dim figure as librarian of an unidentified monastery, was especially concerned with the philosophical works of Cicero, and made from them a collection of selected passages in an order which might well be that of our modern philosophical textbooks. So the whole richness of the thought of the ancient world, preserved in the pages of the *Tusculans*, the *De natura deorum* and the *De amicitia*, was made available to educated men. It might have been expected that a representative of the old school, like Paschasius Radbertus, would rise in protest against the thought that Christians could devote to the interpretation of pagan texts, to Virgil, to Macrobius, time which he himself had kept for commenting on St Matthew. The warning was not perhaps without point. Already the *De praedestinatione* of Erigena, with its profession of faith in the value of reason at the beginning, and its use of texts taken from St Augustine and consciously altered in their meaning, had awakened both the mistrust of those who had thought they could depend on him, and the anger of his opponents.

Now a few years later, in 855, another Irishman, Macarius, having been consulted on the meaning of a difficult passage in the *De quantitate animae*, gave an answer which met with the disapproval of Odo, Abbot of Corbie and future Bishop of Beauvais. He charged Ratramnus with the task of putting this presumptuous young Irishman in his place, and there followed an exchange of writings of which the most important, the second *De anima* of Ratramnus, has recently been rediscovered and edited.

When St Augustine was questioned by Evodius about the number of souls there are, he had admitted his difficulty. He firmly rejected the simple monopsychism according to which there is but one soul for all men. But he could not see how to decide whether individual souls simply exist alongside of one another or whether they are made a unity by their relation to a higher soul. The first seemed to him difficult for a philosopher to maintain, the second possibly beyond the non-Christian's comprehension. Macarius the Irishman, however, had no hesitation: Augustine, in his heart, had adopted the only opinion worthy, in his eyes, of a philosopher; his disciple was thus defending this interpretation against Ratramnus.

Now, how could they have made their own interpretations of St Augustine's hesitation had they not begun to grasp the way in which ideas had developed historically? Something of this can be seen in the teaching of a man like Erigena, for example. Ratramnus, on the other hand, who had no knowledge of Neo-Platonism, badly misinterpreted the problem when he kept the argument strictly to the logical level. According to the monk of Corbie, when Augustine thought of souls as at once many and one he was thinking of the soul as a universal, of the idea of the soul we have in mind when we speak of it, which has concrete existence only in particular souls. The former is an abstraction; only the latter actually exist.

Macarius' pupil, the monk who first asked the awkward question, protests against this interpretation. This gives him the chance of explaining his own at greater length, and of letting us grasp the thread of his argument, which claimed that a universal soul did exist, in which individual souls participate. We are, however, nowhere near the Averroism which Renan thought he found here: that dates only from the twelfth century. This discussion was to have another important consequence. The whole process of Ratramnus' argument, confined to the field of logic, was to centre on the problem of universals, a problem included in and discussed with the aid of Boëthius' *opuscula sacra*. This famous controversy arose earlier, then, than is generally stated. The difficulties were already grasped and posed correctly from the middle of the ninth century. The development of philosophy was thus very much speeded up, and had political circumstances—the break-up of the kingdoms which came out of the empire of Charlemagne, the birth of feudalism, the Norman invasions etc.—been more favourable there is no doubt that the great flowering of the twelfth century would have happened much earlier.

"THE DIVISION OF NATURE"

If Erigena by his teaching helped to start the debate on the universal soul, he himself took no direct part in it. He was then engaged on a task important in a different way. Charles the Bald, devoted as he was to St Denis (Dionysius) the patron saint of Paris, had asked John the Scot to make a new translation of the works then attributed to that saint, who was confounded with the Areopagite converted by St Paul and supposed to have become the first bishop of Athens. The Irish scholar had undertaken the task, and by this long contact with a difficult work had gradually brought his own philosophical thought to maturity. The harvest of this slow ripening was the *De divisione naturae*, a metaphysical system standing so far above the general level of the age that it has been likened to a meteorite fallen from another world, and some have even wondered whether it was not a translation of some Greek work of Pseudo-Dionysius or John Damascene, the original of which has been lost. This last suggestion is too weak to be maintained. However astonishing, the composition of this work was the result of the wide education received by its author, who, like his contemporaries, was of a questioning turn of mind, but who had an extremely unusual and lively intelligence. To this book Erigena added translations of the *Ambigua* of Maximus the Confessor and of the *De hominis opificio* of Gregory of Nyssa, a commentary on the *Celestial Hierarchy* of Pseudo-Dionysius and a commentary on St John's Gospel, only a few fragments of which survive.

What was his object in constructing this system, and what were the means he used?

These are questions much considered in the last hundred years, and very variously answered, because more weight has been given to Erigena's statements on the part to be played by the reason than they really carry in their contexts. From this to making him out a rationalist or a free-thinker is a short and easily-taken step.

John's thought on the organization of the truths of faith by the reason is based on the idea of a hierarchy in the order of knowledge. God has put into man's heart, in giving him reason, an innate need to know the truth. This advance towards the truth he helped by giving us the revelation brought by Christ. This revelation, far from being imposed from without, comes not only to inspire man's mind to action but to lead and guide it to perfection. Erigena takes as his text the words of Christ to the Samaritan woman: "Give me . . . to drink" (John 4. 7). The Lord makes her, already moving towards him, act herself before providing the water which gives life eternal. So with the relation between revelation and human reason. And as this revelation is expressed in the Scriptures, it is by critical acquaintance with and study of these that our minds attain the truth. Philosophy and religion are interchangeable: the former is the application of our mind and reason to the study of the Scriptures, while the latter is nothing other than the submission of all our faculties to revelation. This is what Erigena means when he writes, as early as at the beginning of his *De praedestinatione*, that true philosophy is the same as true religion (*conficitur inde veram esse philosophiam veram religionem conversimque veram religionem esse veram philosophiam*).

Besides *ratio* and *Scriptura* there is also *auctoritas*, which Erigena puts third, and on which he is somewhat harsh. *Auctoritas*, seen in the historical context of the early Middle Ages, is that patristic tradition before which our Irishman refused to bend the knee as unthinkingly as his contemporaries did. True, he expresses the highest admiration for Augustine, Maximus, Gregory of Nyssa and especially "Dionysius the Areopagite", but their authority is only admitted when and if their thought conforms to the demands of reason. What God says, and only what God says, is incontestable, not what various interpreters of his word have later thought. The best proof of this is that they sometimes contradict one another on this particular question or that. So Erigena is by no means a "rationalist" in the modern sense of the word: but he spoke too often of *ratio* and too clearly put *auctoritas* in its place not to be condemned by those who shared his faith and praised by those who had no use for it. On the other hand, he was led by his method of interpreting the Fathers with no other guide but his own intelligence, to reduce them all to a common denominator, Neo-Platonism, and it becomes difficult to distinguish one from another. As Etienne Gilson wittily said: "For amateur heretic-hunters, Erigena is an easy target: one can score a hit first shot. But then one often has to admit sheepishly that in shooting at Erigena one has been shooting at Pseudo-Dionysius, St Maximus the Confessor, St Gregory of Nyssa, St Gregory Nazianzen, St Ambrose or St Augustine."

It has recently been noticed how the *De divisione*, applying this notion of the reduction of everything to Neo-Platonism, is at bottom only another *Hexaemeron*, a commentary on the origins of the world according to Genesis, like those that had been written by all the great writers of Christendom before. But, as distinguished from a St Augustine or a Gregory of Nyssa, Erigena goes back to the very sources of the creative act and considers the problem as part of a general inquiry into the idea of nature. This in fact includes all that we can think of both from the point of view of being and from that of not-being; and it is thus divided into four main parts: nature un-created and creating, which is God; nature created and creating, that is, the Ideas or primordial causes; nature created and uncreating, that is, creatures; nature uncreated and no longer creating, the whole when it has returned to the bosom of the initial unity.

Everything comes from God in order to return to God. That is the unifying thread of the *De divisione naturae*, and the plan of the work is thus not accidental. It is the working out both of the dialectic of nature in its evolution and of the dialectic of man's mind in its effort to attain to knowledge, using as it does two chief means, division and analysis. This last signifies an idea quite different from what we normally designate by "analysis". By division the mind splits an original complex and impenetrable unity into distinct elements; analysis takes up these elements again and progressing from individual to species, from species to genus, from genus to the supreme unity, enables the mind to arrive at a synthesis, all the richer because now it is aware of the richness of the parts thus arranged and ordered. This is the sense in which we ought to take the title of the work, "On the Division of Nature", which does not mean merely classification, but one of the fundamental processes of the mind, these processes themselves being in the likeness of the work of God as it is spread forth throughout the world of his creation.

At this point a difficulty arises: if God is the point of origin of this double process, in the creation and in the mind, how do we get back to that point of origin in the first place? A different process is called for which leads us towards God in two ways: by affirmative and by negative theology. What does this mean? Erigena, in this a disciple of Pseudo-Dionysius, attributes enormous importance to negative theology. It must certainly be admitted that everything we try to say about God limits him in some way to the categories we use. To say of God that he is good, using the same words as we do of ourselves, is the clumsiest approximation. We must, then, surpass these categories, deny these limits. God is not good in that sense. So from negation to negation we are led, not into ignorance, but to true knowledge. God, *qui melius nesciendo scitur*, appears to us then as the *hyperessential* being, according to the terminology so dear to Pseudo-Dionysius; God is he who is more than being: *est qui plus quam esse est*, he who transcends all affirmation and all negation. But then he would be properly unknowable to himself and to us had he not revealed himself from all eternity in a first theophany.

This idea must be properly understood, for it allows of various interpretations, some of which ended in heresy or false mysticism. Theophany is a revelation of God under two aspects, illumination and creation. We only arrive at the full understanding of our own thought when we have given it expression and so brought it into the light; the same is true in a way of God. Incomprehensible to himself in the too-great richness of his unity of being, he had to reveal himself, to unfold that richness. In becoming aware of this he is brought, in a certain way, into existence, and Erigena goes so far as to use in this context the idea of creation: "God creates himself in an ineffable manner in his creation; he manifests himself and from being invisible he becomes visible."

In passing from unity to multiplicity the objects of this divine knowledge are themselves brought into being. The theophany of God has its end in the creation of the noblest of all existents, the Ideas, or primordial causes. So all knowledge ends in the creation of its object, which it projects outside itself. Such is the meaning of the famous phrase: *cognitio eorum quae sunt ea quae sunt est*.

This first creation does not happen in time. It is brought about from all eternity in the very heart of the Word. In him the primordial causes are reduced to unity, for no multiplicity can be introduced into God, but they differ in their effects and are spread out in a hierarchy at the head of which is the Idea of the Good; then comes Essence, or Being, in which all beings subsequently created participate; there follow Life, Reason, Intelligence, Wisdom, Virtue, Beatitude, Truth, Eternity.

This same process of division, by its act of knowing what was, until known, only potentiality, then works in time at all levels of the hierarchy of creatures: those things which are created but uncreating. This is the third stage in the process directed by the Holy Spirit, who multiplies and distributes the blessings of God. At the centre of these lower creatures, between the purely immaterial, the angels, and the purely corporeal, a privileged place is held by man. With man the commentary on Genesis really begins. For properly creation should have stopped with man: as the lowest degree of the intelligible hierarchy, the inverse process of analysis or recapitulation should begin from him. But sin intervened. Like Origen, our Irish scholar regarded sin as producing man's degradation materially as well as spiritually. The division of the sexes and the formation of the world of the body are the consequences of sin. Without sin, the corporeal world would have existed, doubtless, but it would have been unified in the thought of man, a faint reflection across all the successive theophanies of what it is in the thought of God. But after sin was introduced, the physical world came into being in the way in which it now exists. There is nothing odd in the material world's coming from the intelligible world, for everything which exists has its substance and its subsistence only in so far as it is known by the being immediately preceding it in the hierarchy. The physical world has only such solidity as we are able to give it. What would matter be without the categories which we project on to it and which make it intelligible to us?

This explains what has already been remarked on: man's privileged position in the material world. Erigena took up, to express this idea, the already ancient image of the microcosm; but he mistrusted this word and so presented his idea in different words and with a somewhat different meaning. Man is not only a "little world" (*microcosmos*) in the sense that he holds in his body and soul the elements of the whole universe; he is *officina omnium*, the workshop in which all physical creation is produced and in which all nature is thus summed up. Gregory of Nyssa had earlier produced a similar theory, but Erigena provided it with its logical justification by making it a particular case of his general theory of knowledge.

There is no need to go into the consequences of this theory at length. Erigena is a realist in the fullest meaning of the word, since for him Ideas are more substantial than things themselves. The notion of illumination is involved in all the successive theophanies. Each existent thing goes on existing only so far as it expresses the Idea from which it emanates; and it expresses this Idea so far as it contemplates it. Each theophany thus has two effects: creation on one side, contemplation on the other. This is a real Neo-Platonism, perhaps the most complete ever produced by a Christian philosopher. Augustine's Neo-Platonism is strengthened and transcended by the mounting influence of Gregory of Nyssa and, especially, of the *corpus Areopagiticum*, the links between which and Proclus are too well-known to need stressing further.

But this immense process does not stop at man and the physical world. After the division comes the recapitulation, the fourth aspect of nature, the uncreated and uncreating. By sin the multiplicity of beings reaches a maximum and so its highest degree of completion: *informitas* is John's word. The return towards the first unity is first accomplished by man at his death, the last point of division, the first step towards reconciliation. Then comes the resurrection of the body, that is, the reintegration of the physical world in man's mind and its assumption into God by beatification. Division in its last stage is the fruit of sin: recapitulation is the work of grace, which illumines men's minds more and more until it sets them in the full light of God.

But what happens to those who by their sins turn finally away from grace and the possibility of redemption? Erigena, following Origen in this, argued against one form of the belief in eternal punishment; as early as the *De praedestinatione* he could not find sarcasm enough for those who imagined it all too realistically. In the *De divisione* hell cannot be a place at all, for this would make it quite impossible for all nature to return to the original unity. Hell does not exist: there does however subsist in the consciences of the wicked a mark of the supernatural difference between themselves and the righteous: remorse, and ignorance of that Unity which the blessed enjoy.

Such, briefly, is the outline of the vast *De divisione naturae*, the first of the great metaphysical *summae* of the Middle Ages. It is almost unnecessary to add that for a long time it was either unknown or misunderstood. Its use by later heterodox thinkers, indeed, led Pope Honorius III to condemn the book in 1225.

CHAPTER III

THE TWELFTH CENTURY RENAISSANCE

The twelfth century (to which we should obviously join the end of the eleventh) was essentially a period of transition, of discovery. Its rich spontaneity was shown in a thousand new endeavours, establishing Christian philosophy as a definitive science. At the beginning it was to require some effort to restore the level of thought to that at which Boëthius and Cassiodorus had left it, but soon great progress was made and new systems found supporters.

This progress can be discerned even in the teaching methods used. For the earlier masters it was enough to teach grammar and dialectic. Then the complete *trivium* was re-introduced, enriched by a systematic commentary on the Latin classics. Gradually the *quadrivium* received more and more attention. The framework of the seven liberal arts was itself soon left behind and what mattered then was the distinction between the parts of philosophy: to logic were added ethics as well as physics (and metaphysics).

The same may be said of the sacred sciences. At first it was merely a matter of commenting on the Scriptures. Such teaching could clearly be neither synthetic nor systematic. Besides, the pupils urged their masters to provide them with brief outlines carefully constructed so that they might find "what they ought to think" about any question. Thus were brought into being the collections of "Sentences" (*sententiae*, opinions) and the *summae*. In these a logical order imposed itself, and so logic itself was introduced as a means of inquiry; gradually theology became a science, an organized system.

We shall present this development by concentrating, as we have done so far, on the most representative figures, but we can gather the various different sketches into groups according to the most important movements discernible in what these men were doing.

LOGIC AND DIALECTIC: THE QUESTION OF UNIVERSALS

The twelfth century renaissance began with an argument over the nature of universals: "realists" and "nominalists" were opposed not only on the theoretical level but in the theological application of their theories. This made it necessary to discuss the question of the use of dialectic in theology. Despite very firm opposition logic made great advances. The *Heptateuchon* of Thierry of Chartres, a large textbook of the seven liberal arts, written soon after 1140, actually introduces the whole of Aristotelian logic. The reaction among the theologians was to begin to make theology a deductive science in the Aristotelian sense of the word.

As we have said, the problem of universals as the medieval scholars saw it was formulated by Boëthius. Commenting on Porphyry, the Roman philosopher himself wondered what reality could be attributed to ideas of substances. We only perceive individual men, but we have nevertheless in our minds the abstract general concept, man. Should we see in this only an operation of our mental faculties? Are genera and species merely names, only words? This is the nominalist answer. Or should we say that these concepts correspond to ideas existing in a higher world, and that individuals only exist by a participation at once logical and metaphysical in the world of ideas? This is to maintain the real existence of ideas, "realism" in the medieval sense of the word. Plato put these universals in a higher world; the medieval realists set them in the sum of the individuals that are known as a unique reality. Or, lastly, should we consider with the moderate realists that only individuals have concrete existence but the mind has an adequate grasp of their abstract nature, a logical epitome and a metaphysical principle? This is a third answer, already suggested by Boëthius but only fully set forth in the middle of the twelfth century. Before that the problem had to be thrashed out completely in the heated arguments of realists and nominalists.

The realists represented, in the twelfth century, the classical theory, that of the *antiqui*, who enjoyed that prestige accorded to traditional ideas at this period. This is the theory taught, for example, by Odo of Tournai († 1113), who applied it to the human soul and the problem of the transmission of original sin. Each man has in him a part of that unique substance which is the human soul. One individual only differs from another in the accidents of his personal characteristics. This unique substance, stained by Adam's sin, is handed on in that stained state by the begetting of the flesh. St Anselm starts from the same idea to oppose the tritheism of Roscelin: whoever does not understand (he writes in the *De fide Trinitatis*) how a number of men are specifically only one man, cannot understand how a number of Persons, each of whom is God, are only one God. But the best-known supporter of realism is William of Champeaux († 1120), who taught in the cathedral school in Paris, of which cathedral he was archdeacon. In his teaching's original form, before he was compelled to modify it by Abelard's criticism, William taught the theory of the universal essence, which is one and the same in all individuals, contained in all its reality in each. The individual is only an accidental modification of the specific substance.

Opposed to realism was the nominalist theory of the *moderni*, the leader of whom was Roscelin of Compiègne († 1120). Only the individual, he taught, has concrete existence. Genera and species are not realities but words (*voces*) of universal form, mere sounds (*flatus vocis*). Colour does not really exist apart from the particular horse it differentiates from others, wisdom is nothing apart from the soul that possesses it. Unfortunately, Roscelin applied this theory to the mystery of the Blessed

Trinity and refused to allow that a divine nature could exist in three Persons. His retraction of this idea at the council of Soissons in 1092 discredited his theory, but it still found fervent upholders such as, for example, Raimbert of Lille, who argued with the same vigour against Odo of Tournai.

Nevertheless it is true that Roscelin's successors abandoned some of his excesses, and so prepared the way for moderate realism. Adelard of Bath († *c.* 1140) taught a theory of *respectus*, or aspects, as we should say, of being. For him, the same concrete thing is at one and the same time all three, genus, species and individual, but according to different aspects. The first, predominant state is that of the individual reality; genus and species are merely ways of looking at the particular thing, and they are concepts, but not false concepts. They do indicate, above the individual differences, a deeper similarity.

Walter of Mortagne († 1174) uses almost the same idea in speaking of *status*, states. According to different *status*, Plato is an individual (Plato), a species (man), a subalternate genus (animal), and a supreme genus (substance). The first state is real, but the reason gives consistency to the others.

Lastly, we may quote the theory of indifference (*indifferentia*) or resemblance, which was supported towards the end of his life by William of Champeaux, and more strongly by his pupils. Every existent is both different and similar (not different, *indifferens*) with respect to others. The differences are real: they define the way in which each thing is an individual with its own existence. But the resemblances (*indifferentia*) perceived by the mind signify something which is certainly there.

We are thus brought almost to the moderate realism taught by Abelard and Gilbert de la Porrée. These scholars did not cast any doubt on the maxim so beloved by the nominalists: "Only individuals exist", but they considerably reduced the discredit in which the nominalists held the general concept. Indeed Abelard († 1142) showed himself as severe on Roscelin as on William of Champeaux. He reproached the former with not seeing the real meaning of concepts and words, while ridiculing the latter. If every man, Abelard said, is the whole species, man, this is wholly in Socrates at Rome and in Plato at Athens; moreover, Socrates will be present wherever the human species is met with, and at the same moment is in Rome and at Athens. This is absurd.

For Abelard, commenting on Aristotle's logic, the universal concept had more than one aspect, one logical, the other metaphysical. On the logical level there is a kind of nominalism, but one of more substance than Roscelin's. For the term, the word, is actually related to a reality which is signified, and has a logical function. It is essentially a predicate attributed to an individual existent thing to signify its deeper meaning. When I say: "Peter is a man", the only physical reality involved is that of Peter, but the attribute "man" is not simply a word, it does express what is the truth about the subject. And this is where we pass from logic to metaphysics. In fact, Abelard granted to every thing an essence, a nature, common to it and to the other individuals of the species. So the concept does not refer simply to a collection of things, as in the theory of *status*, but to an immanent and intrinsic reality in each individual. Peter possesses the ontological reality of human nature. It is then necessary to admit that the mind does not touch, in the general concept, individual differences, the basis of personality, any more than it exhausts in one word all the reality of the species.

Gilbert de la Porrée (Chancellor of Chartres 1137; Bishop of Poitiers 1142; † 1154), who wrote the *Liber sex principiorum*, a classic of the Middle Ages devoted to the categories of Aristotelian logic, supported similar ideas. By interpreting them in accordance with both the Platonism of Chartres and the *Posterior Analytics*, he deepened their meaning both from the ontological and the psychological points of view. From the point of view of essential reality Gilbert believed that the essence of a thing is the more real because in each individual it is the copy of the divine Idea or pure Form. So he appeals to exemplarism to establish the final form of moderate realism. On the psychological plane Gilbert uses the idea of abstraction. The mind compares the essential characteristics of various things, and then brings about a mental uniting of their resemblances: this common character is what we call the genus or species. This is a matter of a common essence which Gilbert is only too prone to distinguish from the individualized essence. Following out the logic of this unfortunate aberration, the Bishop of Poitiers was led to distinguish a godhead really distinct from the three Persons of the Blessed Trinity. He had to retract this at the council of Rheims in 1148, where he had been accused by St Bernard, to whom he had been denounced by an archdeacon of Poitiers, *Ernaldus Non-ridens*: let us call him Arnold the Serious.

THE USE OF DIALECTIC AND REASON IN THEOLOGY

As may be seen from the last paragraph, twelfth-century writers deliberately carried over their views on universals into theological problems: a fresh indication of "Christian philosophy". But this itself raised a problem: how far are Christians allowed to appeal to dialectic in their study of the data of revelation? On a broader view, have the reason and the philosophers, those who have taught and used the reason, a proper and rightful place in Christendom?

To these questions some writers gave a firmly negative answer. Many names could be cited, such as Gerard of Czanad, Manegold of Lautenbach, and Otloh of St Emmeran; but it seems simpler to gather what is to be said about this attitude—which loses its importance as dialectical theology becomes more and more successful—around three great figures: St Peter Damian, St Bernard of Clairvaux, and Walter of St Victor.

The first was an Italian hermit, born at Ravenna in 1007, who played an important part in the reform of monasticism and the Church under Gregory VII. He was a blunt man fond of expressing himself vigorously:

> I reject Plato, who pries into the hidden secrets of nature; I care not at all for Pythagoras, fixing the limits of the planets' circles, assigning numbers to the movements of the stars, marking out all the zones of the celestial sphere with his compasses. . . .

Let not the orators, after the fashion of Demosthenes, carefully make up their arguments with captious persuasiveness; let them rest in their darkness, all those who are smeared with the filth of earthly wisdom; let them not try, blind as they are in the sulphurous glow of the fog of their learning, to do anything for me. Rather let Christ's simplicity teach me, and may the rustic humility of the truly wise loose the bonds of my doubt.[1]

Peter Damian held that a monk should have nothing to do with the study of the liberal arts, which for him represented all philosophy: a religious should study the Rule of St Benedict rather than that of Donatus the grammarian. Moreover, secular science is useless for whoever seeks the "one thing necessary". If profane learning can render any service to our knowledge of God, it is only as a servant; at all events, the traditional learning has hardly any utility in theology, since God is bound by no rule, the principle of contradiction does not apply in his case, nor did he create secondary causes or natures which have their own proper existence.

It is the more difficult to judge Peter Damian's attitude since it has become the object of argument. Some have wanted to see in it the type of "medieval obscurantism", while others have tried to soften his expressions, even to the extent of forcing the meaning of some passages. To change the words of the *De divina omnipotentia* (Migne, *P.L.*, 145, col. 603 C, D): *artis humanæ peritia . . . velut ancilla dominae*, into *philosophia ancilla theologiae* is not really justifiable. What Christian could deny that profane learning, philosophy as well as history, can play in the study of revelation only an auxiliary rôle? On the other hand, Peter Damian is writing most of the time for monks, and, like many reformers of his time, he thinks that religious should flee the world even in the realm of learning. We have seen before a parallel opposition between the monasticism of St Benedict and Cassiodorus. What perhaps astonishes us most in Peter Damian is his refusal to recognize the existence of natures, essences, in the creation. But surely this is in the tradition of the Old Testament, which, though not

[1] *Ad Leonem eremitam*, c. 1. Migne, *P.L.*, 145, cols. 232–3.

denying the truth of philosophy, does not mention it at all. Secondary causes somehow disappear in the presence of God's almighty power.

St Bernard's attitude is much more refined. He praised the use of profane learning, used his influence to forward the careers of some scholars like John of Salisbury and Peter Lombard, and took care that his monastery of Clairvaux had a well-stocked library including books on all subjects. Yet there clearly remained in his mind a marked reserve with regard to philosophy and its use in theology. Otto of Freising, a Cistercian, tells us that St Bernard was easily inclined to suspicion when thinkers appealed to profane wisdom and human arguments.[2] It is easy to see this in his struggle against Abelard and Gilbert de la Porrée: it was not only a question of a difference of doctrine but of attitude to life and of method in theology. St Bernard considered that for the knowledge as for the service of God the true school is that of Christ, the *schola Christi*, not that in which men learn and dispute with one another. The true science of the monk, that perfect Christian, lies in prayer, reading the Scriptures, meditation and asceticism. He writes to Henry Murdach, master at Paris:

> But do you, my brother, who, as I hear, read the prophets, suppose that you understand what you read? If you do understand, then you know that the meaning of the prophetic declaration refers to Christ. And if you desire to lay hold on him, you can surely attain to him sooner by following him than by reading about him. Why do you seek in the written word the Word who is already here before your eyes, the Word made flesh?... O were I only worthy some time to have you for my companion in the school of piety under the master Jesus!... Believe one who knows: you shall find a fuller satisfaction in the woods than in books. The trees and the rocks will teach you that which you cannot hear from masters.

There is no need either to excuse or to justify St Bernard: his saintliness and his mysticism speak too plainly. No more is there need to plead clumsily a cause which needs no defence.

[2] Otto Fris., *Gesta Friderici Imperatoris*, I. 49.

St Bernard was of those who believe in intuition rather than reason, a search for God through piety rather than the scholarship or wisdom of the intellect. *In domo Patris mansiones multae sunt.* We should not make of him a predecessor of St Thomas, nor should we come close to equivocation by making his idea of monastic theology something comparable to that scholastic theology he tried in vain to prevent from being born at all.

Walter of St Victor was, as Fr Joseph de Ghellinck wrote, "disputatious to the point of injustice". His treatise *Contra quattuor labyrinthos Franciae*, written in 1178, was such as to be described by Mgr Glorieux as "a bad action and a bad work". It is a diatribe against four minotaurs hidden in four labyrinths to prepare the ruin of France, or at least of theology in France. The four are Peter Lombard, Abelard, Peter of Poitiers and Gilbert de la Porrée, whom he reproaches with appealing to the philosophers. The beginning of Book IV is especially significant, containing as it does a lively criticism of philosophers in general and Seneca in particular, Seneca being the favourite author of Geoffrey of St Victor, who was a victim of the ardour of the prior Walter. Why, wrote the latter, why rely on Aristotle and ask him what essences are? Ought not the Stagirite himself to admit that he does not know what they are? Shall we ask him for rules of argument? Their only use is for arguing; now St Paul tells us that a Christian should not love argument. Again, should pagans be able to instruct Christians when it is said in the Gospel that a false brother is to be treated as a gentile and a publican? Walter clearly does not scruple to take the invectives of the Fathers of the Church against certain pagans in a unilateral and exclusive way. According to him, St Augustine, in the end, thought only evil of the Platonists; and the attitude of St Jerome to the classics would be summed up in the famous invective in his letter to Eustochium: "What is there in common between light and darkness? What harmony between Christ and Belial? (2 Cor. 6. 14). What has Horace to do with the Psalter, or Virgil with the

Gospels, or Cicero with Paul? ... We ought not to drink both the chalice of Christ and that of demons."[3]

Opposed to the *anti-dialectici* was the growing number of those who thought it permissible to have recourse to the aid of reason and to the teaching of the philosophers. Sometimes they did this with an audacity normal to those who are reacting against a traditional and authoritative view. This could not happen without serious danger to the faith, as in the case of Berengarius of Tours († 1088), who taught an erroneous doctrine on the Eucharist because he preferred the light of reason to the traditional teaching: *relictis sacris auctoritatibus*, wrote Lanfranc,[4] *ad dialecticam confugium facis*. For Berengarius, it was contrary to philosophy that the eucharistic accidents, the appearances of colour, shape and taste, could be preserved if the substance of bread and wine disappeared. It then became necessary to maintain that the substance of bread and wine remains, that there is thus no real transubstantiation, and that the Body and Blood of Christ are only present in a spiritual manner.

Fortunately, not all attempts to use dialectic in theology were made by such adventurous minds. Even if a proper balance and moderation were not found at once, other attempts were less unhappy in their consequences, being made by saints and greater minds.

The first great name that must be mentioned is that of St Anselm; not only for his personal sanctity, but for the importance he gave to the problem of the relations between reason and faith. His fundamental position is quite clear. Faith and reason are two perfectly sound sources of knowledge. There is no more question of controlling revelation by the reason than of forbidding reason to serve revelation (*credo ut intelligam*) or to work separately towards the same end. But, granted this, it is reasonable to wonder how Anselm's thought ought to be interpreted. When he wrote his *Monologion* he did so in response to requests from some of his pupils and monks,

[3] Epist. XXII; Migne, *P.L.*, 22, col. 416.
[4] *De corpore et sanguine Domini*, c. 7; Migne, *P.L.*, 150, col. 416.

who had been brought up by him to put great trust in philosophy, and who wanted to see the existence and nature of God demonstrated and explained by the reason alone with no argument drawn from the Scriptures. Now St Anselm saw no difficulty in proving in this way the existence not only of the "God of the philosophers", whom, as St Paul said, even the gentiles could know, but the Christian God, the Blessed Trinity, whose existence and nature are a true mystery. And in the *Cur Deus homo?* he tried to demonstrate by the reason the necessity for the Incarnation.

There has been a great deal of argument over Anselm's theory of the relations between faith and reason: some, like Karl Barth, have made of the Abbot of Bec a fideist; others, a rationalist. It seems that really we should allow for an evolution in the thought of the holy doctor, for some uncertainty and irresolution; and we should distinguish, with Sofia Vanni Rovighi, several stages in the thinking of St Anselm on this question. At the first stage, represented by the *Monologion*, of which we have just been speaking, St Anselm really thought that the reason could demonstrate on its own the mystery of the Trinity. He then shifted his ground and corrected his proof for God's existence in the *Proslogion*, using the reason only to confirm faith. Given what the latter tells us of God, how can the reason connect with the deposit of faith? Lastly, St Anselm came to a position much closer to that of St Thomas, asking the reason simply to draw out and discuss the richness of revealed doctrine. This attempt to interpret his thought perfectly conforms with the facts and with the chronology of his writings. It has the further merit of showing that these medieval scholars were real living men whose thought was always developing, whom we should never think of as unchanging fossils.

Whatever may be said of this, we must say something here of St Anselm's proofs for the existence of God, for they have been continually under discussion in the scholastic tradition and in later philosophy. Two proofs must be distinguished: one purely rational, in the *Monologion*, and the other belonging to what we have called "Christian philosophy", in the *Proslogion*; the first *a posteriori*, the second *a priori*, or ontological, to use Kant's word.

Whether it starts from the diversity of goods desired by us, from the values established in the universe, or from the degrees of perfection in creatures, the *Monologion* proof is in all cases based on the idea of participation. We agree, says St Anselm, that there is a great number of different goods. On the other hand, we know that everything has a cause. Has each good a particular cause, or is there but one cause for all goods? The second must be right, for everything possessing more or less of any one perfection does so because it participates in one and the same principle. There must therefore exist a supreme and perfect nature, the source of all good. To be perfect, this nature must be eternal, infinite, immutable, creative, intelligent and free; and it is because this nature must know itself that it is triune: Father, Son and Holy Spirit.

Now this proof, St Anselm thought, might seem too complicated and hardly convincing enough. Would it not be simpler to start from faith and end on rational ground? For we could then start from the idea of God which he has set in us in his image, and which we can never wholly obliterate. Then, it is a matter not of complete penetration of the mysteries of God, but of their comprehension in a certain way. *Neque enim quaero intelligere ut credam, sed credo ut intelligam* (*Proslogion* 1). Now this idea of God in us corresponds to that of a being such that no greater can be thought of (*quo maius cogitari nequit*). Even the impious man who denies God understands the meaning of the word and the idea. So a self-contradiction might arise, for such an idea necessarily implies real existence. Not that a thing conceived is necessarily an existent thing: there is a great difference between a picture imagined in the mind and one actually painted. But in the case of perfect being it would be less than perfect (that is, we should be able to think of a greater) if it did not possess the perfection of existing. Therefore it exists. So it remained for St Anselm to unfold the richness of this perfect nature, both in its creative action and in the life of the Trinity.

We shall not here join in the argument that has gone on since the time of St Anselm himself and his first opponent Gaunilo, monk of Marmoutiers, between supporters and opposers of the ontological argument. But we may perhaps be allowed to draw attention to a historical fact: it seems to us that the meaning of this argument has often been falsified by its being shifted from the religious and theological level to that of strictly rational philosophy. When we read St Anselm's own words, so different from the textbooks' schematic summaries, we gain the impression rather that he wanted to demonstrate that the God we know thanks to revelation is not simply a being who does in fact exist, but a necessary being of whom it would be unthinkable and self-contradictory to imagine that he might not exist. In the context of religious thought and prayer in which St Anselm sets the work in his prologue, it is not a matter of knowing whether God exists, for we speak to him and know him, but of setting forth his perfections: of these the first is necessary existence.

St Anselm is not always easy to understand and interpret; even less so is Abelard. The difficulty is increased because in his case it is not only a matter of deciding the meaning of a thought still feeling its way forward, but also of abstracting from the popular image of Abelard, who has been either over-romanticized, or regarded as a rake and an obstinate heresiarch. Historians have tried in vain to get things in perspective; the popular image remains, clumsy and unfortunate rather than perverted. His affair with Héloïse is always seen in high relief, largely because of the boasting of Abelard himself. But if we give it its proper importance, we are bound to reflect that the sin of a tonsured clerk who later paid for his mistakes by penitence in a monastery was not so great a scandal in an age when the Gregorian reform was finding it difficult to impose celibacy on subdeacons, and there was a large number of married priests. As for Abelard's theological errors, be it remembered that their author made his humble submission to authority, and, after the council of Sens (1141), passed the last months of his life in a state of religious devotion which impressed and inspired Peter the Venerable. Moreover, historians have remarked how many of the texts cited by his enemies either were not really his or were capable of being interpreted in a truer sense, a sense upon which theology finally set its seal of approval. It was so, for example, with the importance of the intention in morals, and with the judgement due to the sin of ignorance. As for the devices used by some of Abelard's adversaries, historians have been reduced to a silence which, according to the temperament of each, betokens indignation or disgust.

Increasingly, Abelard is becoming again for our time what he was in his own, a great Christian thinker, who had numerous followers and warm admirers among popes (Alexander III, for example), cardinals, bishops, theologians and philosophers. For Abelard brought about a decisive advance in theological method. He was already a famous teacher in the field of the liberal arts when a whim took him to study at the feet of the most famous theologian of his age, Anselm of Laon. There he was as dissatisfied by the teaching he heard as he had been with the logic of William of Champeaux. If he did not attack Anselm in the same way, it is because he had by then somewhat moderated his aggressiveness; but criticize him he did, freely, and, with him, the teaching methods he and others then used. Was theology, *scientia divina*, to consist solely in a word for word commentary on the Scriptures, in a compilation of the opinions of the Fathers, the *sententiae*? Would not this be to keep it in a state inferior to that of the liberal arts, the teaching of which was systematic and rational? Some of Abelard's fellow-pupils protested that it was not so easy to comment on the Scriptures, that it was necessary to prepare for it by years of study of traditional interpretations. Abelard replied to them by improvising a commentary on Ezechiel, which roused the jealousy of Anselm, so that he was expelled from Laon, or at least forbidden to teach there. He had no "licence" for Laon, that famous *licentia docendi* without which no one at that time could teach. But when he succeeded in obtaining such a licence at Melun or Paris, he began to present theology in a new way, which stirred his pupils to enthusiasm. Alongside of the commentaries he set forth a systematic study appealing to rational methods, so as to make logical groupings of subjects, to order theological thinking, and enable it to advance by reasoning. How, he asked, could one go on gathering together the sayings of the Fathers, when they were so often contradictory? These give an affirmative, those a negative opinion (*sic et non*). The reason must be appealed to to reconcile them by distinguishing different points of view, as canonists did to clarify apparently differing decrees of different councils. What is more, we should think for ourselves and use our reason to examine the content of revelation. Abelard piles up arguments of this kind in his letter XIII (Migne, *P.L.*, 178, 351) and in Book IV of the *Dialectica* (ed. de Rijk, Assen, 1956, p. 469). The Fathers and St Augustine had used philosophy and dialectic to study revelation the better. St Augustine especially had taught that it was impossible to study the Scriptures without using the reason, and consequently we must study the way reason works to distinguish true from false arguments and to solve difficult problems. It is good and right to have recourse to prayer to understand difficult texts, but, still according to St Augustine, a personal effort must be made to seek the truth by one's own powers (*quaerite et dabitur vobis*) so as to distinguish orthodoxy from heresy, true virtue from its spurious imitation. St Peter says (1 Peter 3. 15, 16) that all Christians must be ready to give an account of their faith. How could they do this without dialectic? Reason and philosophy are gifts of God and therefore good. They too must be made to serve God's glory and be used for the study of his word. If some of the Fathers, popes or councils have been severe against the writings of the pagans, they had in mind the writings of the poets, so dangerous to morals, not those of the philosophers. Lastly, Christ himself is called the Logos by Christians and pagan philosophers alike. This means that he is wisdom itself. Did he not show us this, indeed, in teaching the Gospel and disputing with his opponents? He wanted us, in hearing and living his teaching, in being really Christians, to be in this way perfect philosophers. *Profecto nos pariter Christianos et veros affecit philosophos* (Abelard, Migne, *P.L.*, 178, 355 C).

In arguing in this way, Abelard is alluding to the coincidence of the teaching of the philosophers with that of revelation. He uses the idea freely in regard to the knowledge of God and even that of the Blessed Trinity. In this he shared the illusions about the power of reason of St Anselm and many of his contemporaries. The speculations of the philosophers on the Logos and the World-soul seemed to him to prefigure Christian dogma in the same way as those of the Old Testament on wisdom (see Books I and II of his *Introductio ad theologiam*). If his adversaries criticized him and reproached him with having too much confidence in the philosophers, he replied by stressing their good characters and their real claims on our credence. They were morally good: even St Paul recognizes that they had the natural law in their hearts. They despised temporal goods, and lust and luxury. They prepared themselves by their systematic reasoning for death. Moreover they believed in the immortality of the soul and the judgement to come; and they put moral values first. All that may seem to us very simpleminded. But, to be fair, we must recognize that Abelard steadily moderated his praises of the pagans as he grew older and wrote fresh works in this field. Even in his early enthusiasm he is hardly more prejudiced than the men of the Renaissance and those who have established our courses of the humanities.

We do not need to consider the works written by Abelard and his many followers in the sphere of theology proper. Let us simply remark that the matter of the ten or so theological *summae* which they produced was grouped under the three Augustinian headings of faith (dogma), charity (morals) and the sacraments. Beyond any doubt, they formed a very great contribution to systematic theology, and prepared the way for the extraordinary success of St Thomas in the next century.

If Abelard, the older and wiser Abelard, foreshadows the work of St Thomas, Hugh of St Victor († 1141) represents the movement which blossomed forth and gained authority with

St Bonaventure. It could perhaps be summed up as the predominance of the emotional life. This characteristic can be
plainly discerned, for example, in the study of the faith. For
the Victorine and the Franciscan it is less a question of defining
the place of belief in the hierarchy of modes of knowing, or of
giving a reasonable account of it, than of bringing out clearly
the will to believe and the desire for God that are thus given
expression.

Hugh was from the north, born at Ypres according to some
contemporary sources, or in Saxony according to a later tradition. He came to Paris while still very young, and entered the
monastery of St Victor, founded by William of Champeaux.
The Victorines were not then religious living rather like monks
in a holy retreat remote from the diocesan life of Paris, as they
were to become two generations later. Then they were the most
fervently active section of the diocesan clergy, whose duties
they shared at the same time as they took on those of a more
perfect way of life. One of them was an archdeacon, some were
canons of Notre Dame and others were country priests. The
school of St Victor was then open, in the same way as those of
Notre Dame and Sainte Geneviève, to all students.

While still a young man Hugh became head of this school,
and gave it his particular bias. He wished to steer a middle
course between purely secular studies and anti-intellectualism:
an unstable equilibrium which was not to last long, but the
genuineness of which too many historians have underrated because they have judged the original school of St Victor by that
of the end of the twelfth century, when it was directed by a
mystic like Richard or an anti-dialectician like Walter.

Hugh also had mystical leanings, but they precluded neither
the study of philosophy nor the establishment of scholastic
theology. In his *Didascalicon* he resumes for the most part the
teaching of Boëthius, Cassiodorus and Isidore of Seville. With
them, he regarded philosophy as Christian wisdom; and, as
they did, he drew up a plan of study carefully keeping the
liberal arts separate from the Scriptures. Hugh certainly did
not want to cut out altogether the teaching of pagan authors:

on the contrary, he recommended that they be read and commented on. Of the work of the ancient philosophers it was their logic particularly, and their ethics, that he wanted to be studied. For example, he acknowledged that they had had interesting things to say about the virtues. He was one of the first theologians to assert that there are natural virtues in men, though he was of course bound to demand that they be taken up into the Christian virtue of charity and so brought under the mediation of grace.

In theology proper, he remained firmly attached to the importance of the commentary on the Scriptures, for which he very carefully provided precise rules. But this did not prevent him, towards the end of his life, breaking out of the limits of the old scholasticism and himself writing a systematic, rational *summa* of theological matters, the *De sacramentis*. The scriptural and patristic element is more in evidence than it had been in Abelard, but, as with the latter, reason was present, and present as of right. This conservative spirit which yet blended old and new was to be preserved in the *Summa sententiarum* of (perhaps) Otto of Lucca and especially in the Sentences (*Sententiae*) of Peter Lombard, thus colouring all the theological teaching of the Middle Ages, for this last work was the text commented on in all schools right down to the Renaissance.

In the very first pages of the *De sacramentis* Hugh asserts once again the rightful place of philosophy, in the modern sense of the word. It deals with the work of God in the creation, while theology deals with redemption (*opus conditionis, opus restaurationis*). At the end of the century Geoffrey of St Victor was to draw all the conclusions that follow from this basic distinction. But if Hugh's theological teachings were destined to be surpassed and replaced by the work of the next century, his psychological studies found a better fate. They were used and exploited by theologians and mystics, who saw in them a convenient adaptation of Augustinianism, and who perceived that they made room for introspection and the emotive life in a way that Aristotelianism was never capable of.

Hugh's psychology is strictly Platonic: the two substances, soul and body, are essentially different and their union is only accidental. Yet their union has to be explained both on the level of being and on that of consciousness. The first is done by appeal to a kind of participation which makes matter able to be united to that higher degree of being which is mind. The second is the work of the imagination, which is at the same time a faculty of the intellect and of sense. To understand properly the function which Hugh assigns to imagination, we should think less of the definitions of Aristotelianism or Thomism than of the many-sided concept of modern psychologists. Do they not speak of the creative imagination when they want to talk about the intellect in its highest functions of intuition and discovery, and also of sensible imagination when talking of the most elementary form of knowing?

According to Hugh, the soul thus centred on the imagination has three forms of knowing: sense (*oculus carnis*), intelligence and introspection (*oculus mentis* or *rationis*) and contemplation (*oculus contemplationis*). In the last two distinctions we can see the Augustinian ideas of the *ratio inferior* and the *ratio superior*. The *oculus carnis* has as its object the sensible world. The imagination collects the impressions perceived by the senses; with the help of the reason, it abstracts the essential elements of the realities perceived, and this is how universals come into being, this is their basis. The *oculus rationis* is essentially an introspective faculty: it perceives the life and the reality of the soul, its substantiality, its spirituality, its presence in the body and its action on the latter. It even rises to the knowledge of God, for it perceives itself, as soul, in its contingency, which requires the existence of a necessary being. Moreover, it understands something of the nature of God, since it extends to the supreme being the qualities and values which it perceives in itself. Lastly, the *oculus contemplationis* allows the soul to reach God in himself in mystical union, and to establish a personal relationship with him. Here more than anywhere else, love is bound up with the knowledge which it prepares for and completes.

"PHYSICS" AND PHYSIS

As we have said, learning in the twelfth century was to be found above all in a certain number of cathedral schools: it was to be found in all, it is true, but some of them were more important and had more influence than others. Such was Chartres, the very name of which is used for the most typical development of the age, in metaphysics—or "physics", as it was then called.

The school of Chartres had been founded, or restored, by Fulbert at the end of the tenth century, at almost the same time, that is, as Cluny. But its authority was greatest in the twelfth century, with such masters as Bernard and Thierry of Chartres, Bernard Silvestris of Tours, William of Conches and Gilbert de la Porrée. The curriculum which Thierry set out in his *Heptateuchon* is based on a series of textbooks on the seven liberal arts. But what John of Salisbury tells us of this school, which he knew through William of Conches, shows that this basic education was immediately filled out with a full commentary on texts from the classics and the philosophers. The masters of Chartres, says John, used to explain the ancient writers and then gather the different ideas to be found in them under this or that philosophical heading, logic, physics or morals. Besides this evidence, we have in the manuscript tradition a whole series of works from Chartres consisting of commentaries on the *opuscula* of Boëthius, the *Timaeus* of Plato, the work of one of the Neo-Platonists, or, again, Genesis.

From the point of view that concerns us, the evolution of thought at this time consists essentially of a progressive clarification of the ideas of the divine action and of the nature and mode of existence of created things. The scholars of Chartres began from the theocratic Old Testament conception, whereby beings only exist by the divine will and secondary causes are unknown. They ended, after many attempts and failures and some retracing their steps, at a philosophical picture of the world in which beings have natures which are received from God, it is true, but which are also active principles. At the beginning, God appeared in their work as at once like the Platonic Demiurge and the immanent principle of all things, the World-soul, which has been understood in many different ways and has conjured up the spectre of pantheism. Later, God is really the first cause, both more efficient, because now credited with a truly creative power, and more distinctly transcendent. Indeed, he is involved in created things only in so far as he has given them the principles on which their existence and their action is based.

Bernard of Chartres does not tell us precisely what he thought was the relation between created things and the divine Ideas. Bernard Silvestris often hid his thought in allegory in the *De mundi universitate*, which describes the making, by the divine thought or mind (*Nous*) of the world (*megacosmos*) and of man (*microcosmos*). In Book I, Nature (which is, it is to be noticed, apart from things) complains to God of the chaos in which first matter exists. Providence consents to put some order into the world, and separates out the four elements, using them straightway to make man, the crown of all things.

Thierry, who taught at Chartres about 1121, took the thought of the school into the field of doctrine when he sought to define the four causes of the world. The efficient cause is God; the formal cause is the divine wisdom, the soul of the world; the final cause, the goodness of God; the material cause, the four elements. As can be seen, Thierry did not acknowledge any formal cause intrinsic to created things. These only exist as interpretations of eternal exemplars in the mind of God. Nothing is luminous, he explains, except by virtue of light, nothing hot except by virtue of heat: so created things exist only by virtue of the godhead. That is the form (*forma essendi*) which makes everything exist.

This was also the view of William of Conches when he began to teach. The efficient, formal and final causes of the universe were identified with the Persons of the Blessed Trinity. This allowed him to use an ambiguous phrase dear to his Platonist heart: *mundus non incipit unquam*. Matter, the only cause not divine, began not *in* time but *with* time. We shall

find the same tendency to deny the importance of time, inherited from the Greeks, among the Aristotelians of the
thirteenth century. Besides, William was less interested in the
beginning of things than in their metaphysical status, and for
him the link between the world of immutability and unity and
that of change and multiplicity lay in the activity of the Word,
the archetype or home of the Ideas, and of the Holy Spirit, the
soul of the world and the source of strength and power in the
universe.

But William's thought changed under the influence of two
factors. First, he was the target for the attacks of purists who
smelt heresy in his identification (which was nevertheless
common in the Greek Fathers) of the Holy Spirit and the
World-soul. On the other hand, his philosophical and scientific
knowledge was deepened by his reading Lucretius, Constantinus
Africanus, Helperic and the Arabic writer Honein. He was
thus led to lay still greater stress on the idea of nature, which
he defined as a force immanent in each thing, making it produce
effects similar to itself: *vis quaedam rebus insita, similia de
similibus operans* (*Dragmaticon*, Strasbourg, 1587, p. 31). Even
if William always looked for the first cause of all things and all
characteristics in God, he came later to think that there was in
each thing an intrinsic principle of being and action, which
explains its place and behaviour in the world. These ideas and
phrases were to be taken up and made more precise by later
thinkers: at the end of the century, Alain of Lille made the idea
of nature the very centre of philosophy and moral theory.

It was still necessary to discover and to understand what
sort of thing this *natura* was, how it could be the formal and
intrinsic principle of being and action. This further step was
taken by Gilbert de la Porrée, who was by far the greatest
metaphysician of the twelfth century, and who extended in an
astonishing way Boëthius' teaching on the metaphysical consti-
tution of created things. What Gilbert wanted was to determine
what the *esse* or *essentia* of things was, which made them what
they were, *id quod est*, the substance. From the metaphysical
point of view, that is, considering higher causes, the principle

by which things exist can be none other than God. But from this point of view everything is on the same footing: cats and dogs are both God's creatures. Yet their natures, their *esse*, are different. This is because God determines them by a *subsistentia*, a determinative principle which enables a thing to be, to exist, in this or that way, *esse aliquid*. The substance (*substantia, esse, essentia, natura*) is thus made of two principles, the one *esse*, the other *esse aliquid*. In this way things are explained with reference to God and their participation in the supreme *esse*.

But things can also be thought of with reference to their own nature, as they are in themselves, as those philosophers did who mentally abstracted from the first cause. They laid some emphasis on *subsistentia*, the principle by which the thing has existence (*esse*) and such and such determinate nature (*esse aliquid*). They did not simply say that this substantial principle (*subsistentia*) was an image of the divine Ideas, an effect of God's creative omnipotence. They asserted that *subsistentia* was an intrinsic principle of each thing, its essence, or created nature. This is the viewpoint explicitly adopted by Gilbert in his teaching, so as to demonstrate what things are in themselves. He protested, of course, that he had no desire to encroach at all on what belonged to God: his one wish was to stress, with the philosophers, the immanent character of *subsistentia*.

It can be seen that Gilbert was well aware of the gap between the two conceptions of the world. His use of the terms "theological" and "natural" to qualify these conceptions makes this awareness of his the more significant to us. But, and it is important to recognize this, in his language, "theologians" meant philosophers like Plato, while the *naturales* were writers of cosmologies. Nevertheless, for the Bishop of Poitiers, it was from then on an established thing that the being and action of created things should not be considered only in respect to God but in respect also to the things themselves, their natural principles. The mystics of the time who attacked him and some of his associates were not mistaken about this. Beneath the surface of the struggle which they clumsily waged against certain statements and ideas they did not always properly understand, they were opposing a movement of thought which was gradually establishing the autonomy of the secular and the substantiality of created things. Gilbert de la Porrée might take a firm line with St Bernard, and bring the latter to say that he would willingly dispute with him when he had taught his last class, but he was nonetheless destroying an intellectual "Augustinianism" in which, up to that time, God had been everything. It needed the great genius and authority of St Thomas to set things to rights again by showing that the idea of nature in no way lessens the glory of God but on the contrary magnifies it, for the value of the creature is only the reflection and the effect of the value of the Creator.

MORAL THEORY AND ETHICS

It has for long been believed that the moral theory of the twelfth century was to be found only in theological *summae*, exegetical commentaries or writings of a spiritual kind. We know now that it is also to be looked for in books dealing with *ethica*, the third part of philosophy, according to the division found in all medieval writers.

What led to such a mistake being made was the fact that *ethica* is not included in the list of the seven liberal arts. But we should never forget a fact which is always true of medieval authors: they were not slaves to their classifications. They added the broader classification of the three parts of philosophy to that of the seven arts, as we have seen more than once already. Moreover, the two lists of disciplines could easily be made into one, especially by the mediation of *grammatica*. This was not only concerned with giving theoretical rules, but studied and commented on classical authors. It was enough to include among these works some on moral theory, or passages concerned with the subject, and *grammatica* found itself dealing with ethics. To a lesser degree, rhetoric could do the same. Masters like Thierry of Chartres and Manegold of Lautenbach

commented on the rhetoric of Cicero. Now Cicero, writing of
the deliberative kind of oratory, includes a brief statement of
moral theory consisting mainly of a classification of the virtues.
This classification was as popular with twelfth century writers
as that of Macrobius.

So it is easy to see both that their ethics were authentic and
that they were limited. The writers of this century were not
concerned to establish a separate moral theory abstracting from
the supernatural end of man. What they wanted to do was to
rebuild the ancient pagan ethic and set it in a higher, Christian
synthesis. Hence this ethic is found at two levels in the schools
and their curricula: teachers of rhetoric and grammar studied
it in the courses on the liberal arts, and theologians, and even
mystics, made room for it in their teaching also. From the beginning of the century, writers on ethics recognized both the
usefulness, or even necessity, of this reference to pagan
moralists, and the unequal value of what these had to offer.
Hugh of St Victor draws a distinction between ethics, begun
by Socrates and studied in the works of Plato and Cicero, and
moral theory, drawn from the writings of St Gregory the Great.
Abelard sets beside the *ethica* of the pagans the *divinitas*
(theology) of the Christians.

The point of departure for this study is thus the reading of
and commentary on the ancient works on moral theory.
Alexander Neckam gives a very full list of such works: among
them are the *Disticha Catonis*, Virgil's *Aeneid*, Seneca's letters
(the Seneca about whom the Victorines argued, as we have
said), Juvenal's *Satires*, Horace's poems and some of Ovid's,
and Cicero's *Tusculans, De amicitia, De senectute* and *De
officiis*.

How were these works studied and, if we may put it so,
exploited? By various methods, which sometimes overlapped
even in the works of the same author. The simplest and
apparently most logical was that of the continuous commentary.
The master explained the text of Cicero or Ovid word by word
and remarked on its content. Very often he resorted to allegorical methods, which were thus as common in arts studies as

in Biblical exegesis. In a time when every text, even from a profane author, represented a venerable authority, the allegorical
method offered the advantage of freedom: thanks to it, one
could saddle an author with all that one wanted to say oneself,
or in any case make him appear to say what he did not in fact
say, if one happened to disagree with him. This had the effect
in the field of ethics of making Ovid a teacher of morality, a
particularly droll thing for us with our modern sense of history.

But this method of commenting on the texts seems to have
been less popular than that of making anthologies (*florilegia*).
These grouped together according to a traditional plan or the
personal ideas of the anthologist a series of texts culled from
all sorts of sources. The most famous is the *Florilegium Galli-
canum*, which quotes moral maxims and texts under the names
of the authors to whom they were attributed. So we find a
whole series of moralizing quotations from Horace, for
example, on the thought of death, on poverty, on conjugal
harmony, on drunkenness, and so on. Other anthologies, such
as that of Oxford, were built on a logical framework, that of
the four cardinal virtues.

Similar to these are the works belonging to the tradition of
Chartres; but in these the author's part is greater, for we move
on from the logically arranged *florilegium* to the original work
enriched by a multitude of quotations. According to John of
Salisbury, Bernard of Chartres encouraged his pupils to list
and to regroup passages in the authors they studied dealing
with philosophy, and especially with moral theory. John's own
teachers, William of Conches and Richard Lévêque, imitated
Bernard, and he himself tried to follow his inspiration. Tradition has in fact handed down to us a *Moralium dogma*
attributed to William, which is essentially an adaptation of
Cicero's *De officiis* made up of a long series of short quotations. In it the author teaches the future Henry II of England,
whose master he was, to choose the good that is right rather
than the good that is useful or profitable, and defines for him
the duties of prudence, justice, fortitude and temperance. As
for John of Salisbury, he sets out first a fundamental theory of

morality based on the ideas of the good and of virtue, and then man's particular duties under four heads: the inquiry into what is the proper good, respect for one's neighbour, one's religious attitude towards God, and contempt for the world. He ends his work with some pages the more precious because so rare for that time, on private and political morality.

Not all the adaptations of the ancient writings made the same use of such quotations, which the students of that time used to learn by heart. When Aelred of Rievaulx took up the *De amicitia* he wanted to produce a more original, religious work: he wanted to transpose the teaching of Cicero on friendship into a Christian form. His work found numerous imitators and was itself adapted and reshaped, especially by Peter of Blois, who earned the name "king of the plagiarists" at a time when such borrowing was extremely common. A canon of Oxford, who seems to have been influenced by the Victorines both in his religious life and in his theological leanings, rewrote with considerable dexterity the part of Apuleius' *De Platone* concerned with moral theory. He thus produced a little treatise of general moral theory directly inspired by that work of the second century of our era, built up around the idea of the goods that man can seek, the virtues by which he attains them and the faculties he uses in the seeking. Here again, as in Cassiodorus, the treatise on man is intimately bound up with morality.

Lastly, there is another source from which twelfth century writers drew their knowledge of the ancient ethics, the Fathers. An attack on marriage made by the Neo-Platonist Porphyry and used by St Jerome in his dispute with Jovinian, who denied the virtue of virginity, was thus made available to the medieval writers, who recopied, worked over and rewrote it to their hearts' content. The summary of basic Platonist ethics which St Augustine had included in his *City of God* was Abelard's immediate source for his *Dialogue between a philosopher, a Jew and a Christian*, and John of Salisbury's for his criticism of Epicureanism.

What were the results of all this on the ethics taught in the schools? What sort of ethics came from this study of the pagans? There was certainly no question of a complete revolution, nor of an unconditional return to the ideas of antiquity. But this does not mean that ideas were not given a new and different expression, nor that the duties of man and the virtues were not seen in quite a different light. Certain Biblical ideas never appeared: that of the Law, for example, or the evangelical idea of the imitation of God and of Christ. These writers never insisted that man, the image of God, ought to reproduce his exemplar. In a sense we can say that, although God was often mentioned, this ethic does not begin with God but with man. It was a matter of giving man his proper value by turning him towards the true good, by encouraging in him true virtues, by developing his faculties towards true greatness. It was not a matter of a dialogue between God who calls and man who answers, as in the Bible. This is why these writings on moral theory give so little space to the idea of sin, the breaking of friendship with God and the refusal of obedience. If they speak of these things, it is when they leave their pagan sources and go back to the Christians, especially to St Gregory. In the logic of their system, a moral failing is more of an error than an evil will; they had more regard for man who destroys himself than for God who is mocked.

The same contrast can be seen when we look at what they had to say about the virtues. The theologians and spiritual writers of the age quote, among others, the Gospel virtues, according to the list of the beatitudes or the gifts of the Holy Spirit. The teachers of ethics make no mention of them, but stick to the moral virtues, the subdivisions of which, drawn from Macrobius or Cicero, are of tremendous concern for them. There is no opposition here, only a difference of perspective, except perhaps so far as concerns certain ideas which scarcely occur in the Gospel, such as the ordered love of oneself, or magnanimity, or self-defence. Here again man seems more important.

Lastly there is one final characteristic of this ethic that must be described, however briefly, simply to bring out its wealth of content. This is the production of historical accounts of customs and behaviour, empirical psychological observations, which were full, varied, and very numerous. They formed the basis of a moral theory which was perhaps rather down-to-earth, but on the other hand was full of detail and very realistic, and which certainly is very valuable for the history of ideas. There is less divergence here from Christian ideas than in the case of statements on the good or on virtue, for this was stuff that could be informed by *caritas* as well as by *cupiditas*, if we may use here the Augustinian distinction. It was a sort of common sense, of prudence rich in experience, opening up sometimes for the careful reader views full of interest on an age which knew more of the subtleties of character and of humour than we think.

All this work on ethics was not without great influence on moral theology. And once again we must stress that what we today call philosophy and theology were intimately mingled in the twelfth century, so that we cannot study their ethics without also consulting their theological works.

Dialectic brings about a first meeting of philosophy and theology in ethical matters. What happened in the cases of original sin or the dogma of the Trinity also happened in that of moral problems. Alongside of the Biblical ethic, which was to keep its place of honour down to the fourteenth century, there were appearing the first signs of a systematic or rationalized moral theory taking its principles from revelation or from a philosophical idea accepted by Christians, and then being developed and expounded with all the vigour of men's reason.

St Anselm sketched out a general theory of ethics in his two treatises, *De veritate* and *De libertate arbitrii*. If the second foreshadows the *De actibus humanis* of the *Prima secundae* of St Thomas, the first poses the problem of moral obligation. For the Abbot of Bec, truth is not only in the mind, it also issues in action; it consists in rectitude and justice, that is, in the conformity of man's action with his personal dignity and his creaturely condition. A Johannine idea (8. 44) is here interpreted in philosophical terms.

Abelard also had recourse to dialectic in writing his Ethics, the *Scito teipsum*. Here again we have an approach to a treatise on human actions, for he is discussing and arguing about the imputability of acts. Abelard wanted to combat—he was a born fighter!—the moral theory of his time, which was often objectivist in the bad sense of the word: his contemporaries saw in an action more the brute fact than the psychological conditions which caused it. The "material sin", as we call it today, counted for almost as much as the fault of the will. Abelard therefore reasons, analyses, divides, so as to show that more importance should be attributed to the intention, to the personal element. He piles up moral arguments to establish this, in which he belongs to the Augustinian tradition. But how awkward he sometimes is, how he twists and turns, and how he exaggerates. His boldness frightened many people off, but this did not prevent the idea he stressed so much gaining more and more ground as theologians made considerable use of his work. This is true, moreover, not only of the theologians in the schools but of those in monasteries also. Many monks, of course, were well-educated, and they had not for the poets and moralists of antiquity the same horror that they felt for logic. So the Cistercian Thomas of Perseigne contrived to insert in his *Commentary on the Song of Songs* and in his *De praeparatione cordis* several hundreds of quotations from the ancient moralists, who, to his mind, ought to bring their support to the authority of the Scriptures. A passage of Wisdom on envy, for example, leads him to quote four passages from the poets on the same subject. Helinand of Froidmont, also a Cistercian, did the same sort of thing in his *Flores*, which achieved some fame, for they inspired Vincent of Beauvais, the Dominican who in the following century had charge of the education of the sons of St Louis. In this work or that, the same quotations, the same names occur. We can only mention here, very briefly, Helinand's attitude to Socrates and the *gnôthi seauton*: disregarding a good many distinctions, he sees in the philosophical method of Plato's master an appeal to the interior life, the life of prayer.

Ethical considerations occur just as constantly in the works of the theologians of the schools. When the *summae* began to appear, there was hardly one which did not include the four cardinal virtues and their innumerable ramifications. At the end of the century, Peter the Cantor was still more accommodating, for in his *summa* of moral theology, *Verbum abbreviatum*, he does the same as Thomas of Perseigne and quotes the pagans very freely. This was to bolster up his doctrinal teaching and to adumbrate a casuistry. As we know, he was the leader of a school of theologians who, at the end of the twelfth century, were distinguished by their desire to give the most complete treatment of ethics, in its three aspects, Biblical, theoretical and pastoral.

Many doctrinal points deserve to be mentioned, but we must be content with two examples in which the conjunction of ethics and moral theology is particularly significant.

The first concerns the coming together of the philosophical and the Christian teaching on virtue. As we have said, there was hardly a theological *summa* which did not give a prominent place to the lists of virtues of Cicero or Macrobius. But this was done in such a way that these virtues had no value for a Christian unless they were taken up into charity. Let us take two *summae* of the school of Abelard: the *Sententiae Parisienses* and the *Sententiae Hermani*. The order of presentation of the subject is identical in the two works. Moral theory begins by setting out the idea of virtue, as centred on charity. Then follows the consideration of the contrary, that is, vice and sin; and it ends with an examination of merit and its conditions. In short, we find here united our modern treatises *de caritate, de virtutibus, de peccatis et vitiis*, and part of *de actibus humanis*. These disciples of Abelard do not set about things as do modern authors, giving first a definition of virtue in philosophical terms, and then its application to the moral order and to theological graces, rather more successfully in the first case than in the second. For them, virtues only exist at all in dependence on charity, as its manifestation and realization in practice. It is only when they have dealt with charity that they mention the other virtues. Indeed, they explicitly say that all virtue is charity, or that charity is the basis of every virtue.

Alain of Lille, in the *De virtutibus et vitiis* written about 1160, in which for the very first time the term *theologia moralis* is used, asked what status these philosophical virtues had. Had they any for the Christian? Did they bring any merit? Or could they become such as to confer merit? He was well aware of the distinction between the two kinds of virtues, as of the possibility of raising them from the state of nature to that of grace. All depends on their basic motive: it is enough to do for love of God what one has previously done from natural instinct. From the Christian point of view, every good action is the fruit of collaboration between nature and grace. Free will is as it were the power in the seed that produces the plant when watered by the rain from heaven.

In the same author we find an idea strongly stressed which was then very important in moral theory, that of the natural law. True, the Middle Ages were full of references to the natural law, but these were mostly in Augustinian terms which profoundly affected its meaning. St Augustine, in fact, wanted to answer the Pelagians, who denied the necessity for grace; so he asserted that when St Paul attributed to pagans the knowledge and practice of the natural law, he meant converted pagans who had accepted the grace of faith. From this to saying that the real natural law is that of the Gospel and the Law of Moses, is only a step, one which the canonists eagerly took with Gratian, the author of the *Decretum*.

But all this had nothing to do with those who had read the books of Cicero or who were, like the scholars of Chartres, restoring the idea of nature. Alain of Lille, who owed much to Gilbert de la Porrée, constantly emphasizes the idea of nature, especially in his works on ethics, the *De planctu Naturae* and the *Anticlaudianus*. In the first, nature, personified, condemns sodomy and reminds us of the natural laws of physical love, and goes on to attack the other vices, which are similarly distortions of nature's own ideas. In the second, she undertakes to form, by virtue of her office as vicar of God, *vicaria Dei*, a perfect man. To do this she calls for aid to her sisters, the sciences and the virtues, governed by Prudence on the worldly level, by Theology on that of grace.

So we see that restoring the idea of nature in the realm of physics had as a parallel its establishment in moral theory. On the level of cosmology, nature was seen as an instrumental cause, in the hand of the almighty Creator. She was charged with keeping the law of genera and species according to the divine exemplar and with operating the dynamic power which God has inserted in the heart of created things. Why should it be different in the case of man? Nature's task is more difficult to accomplish because account must be taken of free will; and it is thereby a more noble task. But the idea is the same. Nature is a kind of mouthpiece for the voice of God, driving man to realize himself according to the demands of his own essence. So she demands of man all those virtues by which his mind and heart can really be what they ought to be. Nature also has a social function: she desires that man worthily take his part in the propagation of the species. It is to go against her laws to seek sexual satisfaction while refusing to accept the responsibilities it implies in the creation of new lives. So there is in Alain a reaction against the pessimistic views of Augustinianism on marriage, and a vehement condemnation of sodomy, a sin against nature in the fullest sense of the words.

CHAPTER IV

THE AGE OF SCHOLASTICISM, OR THE ARISTOTELIAN AGE

It is always dangerous to try to sum up a whole period in one word, for there is a very great risk of over-simplifying a complex reality. Yet we may perhaps be allowed to emphasize the dominant characteristic of an age and headline the problem with which it was most preoccupied. In this spirit we may say that the thirteenth century was the period of the invasion of Aristotle and of Arabic philosophy. In a great wave, as it were, they swept away the old Christian Neo-Platonism and reverence for the classics, with the idea of practical wisdom which this implied. The intellectuals of the age began to discover the Aristotelian synthesis, rich in both the scientific and the philosophical fields. Contemporary writers made no mistake: one of them, the trouvère Henri d'Andeli, rightly spoke of the "Battle of the Seven Arts", and in his poem portrayed the new teachers attacking the old positions to capture them by main force.

For this change was certainly not brought about without some searching of consciences or without arousing some reaction. We might perhaps be tempted to judge this reaction too harshly, because we know what course history took, and also because we ourselves live in a time of evolution and change. Yet it had its proper part in the story, for it acted as a check on this movement of ideas and, by preventing excess, made possible the creation of a new synthesis, itself rich in ideas.

We shall treat in turn: (1) The new philosophical sources; (2) The introduction of Aristotelianism into philosophy and theology; (3) The Franciscan school; (4) The Dominican school and Averroist Aristotelianism.

THE NEW PHILOSOPHICAL SOURCES

Up to the end of the twelfth century, Christian philosophy was nourished on the thought of the Fathers, on the classics and on the work of compilers like Boëthius and Cassiodorus, who handed down to later ages part of the antique heritage. In these sources this philosophy found an intimate union between Christian revelation and a Neo-Platonism seen through Christian eyes. And it was this which characterized Christian philosophy.

But now the men of the west gradually began to know the Aristotelian *corpus*. Now they were dealing with a great work of synthesis which had nothing Christian about it, neither in the thought of its maker nor in any interpretation of it made later. The medieval scholars were far even from suspecting what we know now about the evolution of Aristotle's thought, which passed from metaphysics to the strictest empiricism. Yet they could not but see that, even taking into account the writings of the time when Aristotle was still following Plato in his belief in a single God, the Stagirite attached very little importance to his "prime mover". His universe was like that of modern science, which refuses to look towards a beyond but closes itself on itself. Moreover, while Platonism had been the philosophy preferred by the Fathers, they had stigmatized Aristotle as an enemy of the faith; in no way had they tried to adapt or adopt his system.

Paradoxically, it was by the influence of the Moslem Arabs that a bridge was found between these very different two worlds of thought, and the work of assimilating Aristotelianism begun. We have indeed to wait until the second half of the century to see the whole *corpus* of Aristotle's works translated direct from the Greek; in this regard, William of Moerbeke was to render

St Thomas most important service. But much earlier than this his writings began to be known, thanks to the translations, adaptations and commentaries made by Jews and Arabs. The geographical points of contact at that time were south Italy and Spain, where Christians and Moslems lived side by side.

The first of the great names we must at least mention here is that of Avicenna (Abu 'Ali al Hosain ibn 'Abdallah ibn Sina, c. 980–1037) of Bokhara in Persia, a philosopher of immense literary output. He it was in particular who provided the Latin west with a vast compilation of Aristotelianism, through the mediation of translators of Toledo gathered around the archdeacon Gondissalvi (Gundissalinus). In fact, like so many other medieval scholars, Avicenna made up Aristotle's philosophy with some Neo-Platonism, especially that which he found in a work falsely attributed to Aristotle, the *Theology*, which was in reality composed of extracts from Plotinus.

Avicennism spread among the scholars of the Latin west the ideas of the real distinction between essence and existence and of matter as the principle of individuation, and raised the question of the active intellect.

Pressing the Aristotelian distinction between act and potency, Avicenna taught that with the exception of God, the One, everything is in itself merely possible or contingent: it has no existence in its own right, but must receive its existence from a first cause. In the case of sensible things, this composition presupposes another, for the form is not individualized by itself. Only descent into matter brings about the divisibility of a form, which in itself is universal. In our world, the ingrafting and multiplication of forms is the work of the active intellect, the soul of the sublunary sphere and the tenth emanation from the supreme One.

Clearly, the case of man is particularly complicated, for his form transcends matter and is capable of knowing immaterial things, the universals. According to Avicenna our knowledge passes through four stages, only the first three of which properly belong to us. After the first stage, sensation, the imagination achieves a first, sensible abstraction, and then the soul perceives particular, non-sensible ideas. It remains to attain to the knowledge of general ideas. This is too difficult for a soul sunk in matter and the possible intellect is insufficient. It is thus a task reserved for the active intellect of the species, which thereby takes on a second rôle in the universe.

Things were worse still with Averroes (ibn Roschd, 1126–98), who got rid of all Neo-Platonic influence and kept strictly to Aristotle. In the spirit of his system he is even anti-religious, and sets philosophy firmly above theology: this last is sufficient for the ordinary man, but the true knowledge of things, in the deeper sense of the term, is reserved for the philosopher.

The god of Averroes is no longer involved in an emanation which, by bringing him down, sets him in contact with all beings. He becomes once again pure act, far removed from the world, which governs itself and develops itself in the generation of species. For Averroes, the forms of sensible things no longer even come from the active intellect; they are produced by the play of natural forces. The only concession Averroes made to religion, or rather in fact to Moslem theology, was to say that God created the world. But he at once declares that this creation was eternal and necessary, so that his God is neither involved in nor degraded by the unfolding of its history.

Following out the logic of his Aristotelian empiricism, which he accentuates by making the suggestions and doubts of the Stagirite into firm assertions, Averroes is led to the conclusion that the human soul cannot be at the same time the form of the body and a spirit. Since it animates matter it must itself be material and mortal. What spirituality Avicenna had left it, the possible intellect, capable at least of conceiving the ideas with which the active intellect presented it, is now confined to the level of the species. There is only one active intellect and only one possible intellect for the whole human species; and these make their appearance and carry on their work in each individual man.

We know that such theories as these aroused great suspicion when they were introduced into the schools of Paris at the

beginning of the thirteenth century, provoking radical condemnations in 1210 and 1215. Aristotelianism and all that there
was of good in it was compromised by those very authorities
and scholars who were making it known and who presented
their interpretation as the only valid one. With time, a more
moderate solution was adopted: Pope Gregory IX, while
confirming the preceding condemnations, declared (April 3rd,
1231) that they would not apply to the expurgated texts of
Aristotle which a commission was to establish. This work was
never finished, and perhaps could never have been finished.
Aristotelianism had to be rethought in a Christian way. This
was to be the work of the masters of the young universities and
the mendicant orders.

THE INTRODUCTION OF ARISTOTELIANISM

For keen and vigorous forces were mustering for the attack
on the citadels of learning. The thirteenth century showed for
"philosophy" the same enthusiasm as the eighteenth for "enlightenment" and the nineteenth for "science". Masters and
students had become aware of their strength. They overcame
their desire for independence and autonomy and federated
themselves into a huge corporation which, being more famous
than the rest, took to itself the name given at first to each and
all, *universitas*.

As to relations with the bishop and his chancellor, the
masters had obtained the right to fix the conditions for licences
(*licentia docendi*), which meant they had control of the actual
teaching. They alone awarded the status of bachelor (vavasour,
or assistant teacher) and doctor (master). As to the civil power,
the university formed a real state within the state. For masters
and pupils were clerics: many were satisfied with the tonsure
alone, never receiving even minor orders. Now clerics were
exempt from the king's justice, their cases belonging only in
the ecclesiastical courts. A long strike on the part of the scholars
forced the Regent of France, Blanche of Castile, to translate
these claims into fact.

As for the teaching itself, we have now progressed far from the scattered and disordered efforts of the twelfth century. Curricula became more specialized and were carefully arranged. At Bologna, Montpellier and Paris especially, where the schools, now federated, had become universities, students were now divided among several different faculties. At about fourteen the student entered the arts faculty, where he was to study for four years. There he deepened his knowledge of grammar, which he had begun in some "primary" school, and added rhetoric to it. Then he gave a good deal of his time to dialectic and logic. Lastly, he started on metaphysics, ethics and the sciences. It was the Aristotelian *corpus* which supplied the greater number of books commented on by his teachers, either in a rapid manner (*cursorie*, whence our word "course") or more profoundly.

As a young master of arts the student then went on to another faculty, medicine, law or theology. The last has particular interest for the historian of medieval Christian philosophy, for the masters who taught theology often "determined" problems of metaphysics, psychology, cosmology or ethics. They were, as we have seen, only following the tradition of six centuries; nor did they feel they were going beyond their proper field, for it was under their theological aspect and in their relations to revelation that these questions were examined. This is why scholastic philosophy, at the present day, finds its schemes and methods more often in the works of the thirteenth century theologians than in those of the art professors. Besides this, it must be noticed that among the most vigorous thinkers of the century were a number of Dominicans and Franciscans. Now these new religious orders, full of zeal for knowledge as well as for their apostolate, intended that their masters should remain first and foremost theologians, and did not allow them to teach in the arts faculty, which was more secular, more worldly, than the others.

At first sight, it is true, it would seem that the curriculum of the faculty of theology made very little room for philosophy.

The pupil began by following for two years the courses given by a bachelor licensed to lecture on the Scriptures, and then for the same length of time listened to a commentary from one licensed to teach from the *Sentences* of Peter Lombard. Then for three months at least he heard the lectures of a master who took up the Scriptures again with a more profound exegetical commentary. This seems to have been more a matter of what has been called since the sixteenth century positive theology than of scholastic theology. In fact, the commentaries both of the lecturer on the *Sentences* and of the master offered a good deal of scope to the reason and independent thought, whether it was a question of theology or of philosophy properly so-called. Moreover, the regular courses were supplemented by questions and disputations which were exclusively philosophical and rational in their method and often in their matter also. Think for example of the great richness of the teaching in St Thomas's *quaestiones ordinariae*. The only scholastic books specifically excluded from the curriculum were the theological *summae*, the masters' personal syntheses. Theoretically, these were works of reference and for private reading, where the pupil could go to see how all fitted together and to further his education. One has only to read the most famous prologue of them all, that of St Thomas, to be sure of this. But, truth to tell, very often important parts of these *summae* were used in practice by their authors, and still more by their pupils, in a commentary on the Scriptures or on Peter Lombard. If it is true that the Thomist *Summa theologiae* did not become an official textbook until the sixteenth century, yet it is none the less true that from the end of the thirteenth Dominican teachers often consulted and used it in their exegetical courses.

Among the first theologians to make much use of Aristotle despite their theoretical opposition or at least mistrust, were three masters of the Paris theological faculty: William of Auxerre († 1231), Philip the Chancellor († 1236) and William of Auvergne († 1248). These were not satisfied simply with taking from the Greek philosopher a method of reasoning, but referred to the actual content of his teaching and that of his Arabic commentators in setting out ideas which were specifically philosophical.

Philip the Chancellor, for example, was the first to write a treatise on the transcendental properties of being (unity, truth and goodness) in a spirit which goes back both to Aristotle's metaphysics and to the Neo-Platonism of Boëthius and Pseudo-Dionysius and, indeed, of Avicenna. He gave fresh life to the treatise on the conscience by introducing the theory, thenceforth classical, of the *synderesis*, the *habitus* of the first principles of action, analogous to the *intellectus*, the intellectual faculty which knows, as it were intuitively, the first notions of rules of being. Philip was quite as clearly influenced by the new movements when he tried to make a synthesis of the Augustinian tradition of the spirituality of the soul and the Aristotelian idea of the soul as the form of the body.

As for William of Auvergne, he gave pride of place to Avicenna, even if he criticized or even opposed him on occasions. His attitude reminds us of St Ambrose, who practically copied Cicero in his *De officiis* yet never lost a chance of reproaching him. When William deals with the distinction between essence and existence which is characteristic of every created thing, he quotes Boëthius, but it is obvious that he interprets Boëthius by means of Avicenna. *Esse* and *id quod est* are no longer, in fact, essence and individual, as in the Christian philosopher, but nature and the act of existence as in the Arabic thinker. Master William used Avicenna, without saying so, in defining God as necessary being and thus laying the foundation for the natural knowledge of God. But he expressly criticizes Avicenna's idea of necessary and mediated creation, though for this topic he uses another Arabic writer, the Jew Avicebron (ibn Gabirol, *c*. 1020–70).

If we want to see the progress first made by Aristotelianism in an arts faculty, we have to look to Oxford, where the prohibitions of Paris were never effective. Very early in the century, Alfred of Sareshel commented on the Stagirite's works on physics, especially the *De meteoris*. John Blund, about 1230, produced a *De anima* inspired by that of Gundissalvi, though surpassing his in subtlety of thought. Adam of Buckfield, also, commented on almost all the works of Aristotle and proved himself a faithful follower of Averroes.

English Aristotelianism really reached its maturity with Robert Grosseteste, chancellor of Oxford University before becoming Bishop of Lincoln. It was no longer presented in an imitative fashion but thought out afresh and further developed partly by a zeal for personal inquiry which was rare at that time, partly by a Neo-Platonist metaphysics. We might compare the work of Grosseteste, like that of many authors of syntheses of the thirteenth and fourteenth centuries, to a stratified cone. Its base, which forms a large part of it, is essentially scientific and cosmological Aristotelianism. The next higher stage is given over to the humane studies of psychology, ethics and metaphysics: here Aristotelianism is crossed with Neo-Platonism, Augustinianism and the data of revelation. Lastly, the topmost part of the cone is theology properly so-called, and, taken up into it, a philosophy that is Aristotelico-Platonic, and sometimes more Platonic than Aristotelian.

In one sense Grosseteste was very modern: an important part of his teaching, the echo of which is to be heard in his immense literary work, was given to scientific observation, which he interpreted with the help of mathematics. It seems that the phenomenon of light particularly struck him, so that he wanted to carry its interpretation into philosophy and even into theology, where he found, beside analogous Augustinian ideas, expressions in the Gospel of St John of the same tendency. For him, God is light, above all, and other beings are lights only by participation, composed as they are of act and potency, of matter and form. Light is a substantial element penetrating bodies, which, spreading through prime matter, confers on it spatial extension. *A fortiori*, spirit is light; and knowledge is an irradiation of the uncreated Light in which we see the truth of things.

When Robert Grosseteste finished teaching in 1235 to

become Bishop of Lincoln, his pupils Roger Bacon, Adam Marsh and Thomas of York carried on the torch. It was the first of these, Roger Bacon, who introduced into Paris, during his stay on the Continent about 1240, the practice of commenting on all the works of Aristotle, taking no further notice of the old prohibitions. This professor of the arts had a truly original mind; he was to enter the Franciscan order in 1256, to enjoy the favour of a pope, and then to spend many years in the prison where his bold, not to say revolutionary, ideas had brought him. For him, the common active intellect could only be God, who enlightens every man and gives him wisdom. Some men have been granted a special enlightenment: they are the sacred writers and the philosophers, at least in regard to some of their statements. But all enjoy this divine light which enables them to see the truth and to grasp all the better the meaning of concrete existents. In these last, moreover, we encounter the universal divine power, the genus and the species, which are immanent forces rather than *entia rationis*. So the Augustinian illumination, the Aristotelian-Arabic idea of the active intellect and a kind of nominalism are all joined in a curious way as the basis for a profound interpretation of the concrete world and of history.

ST BONAVENTURE

Another Englishman teaching at Paris was also to don the habit of St Francis and, by bringing a chair of theology into his order, to encourage the movement favourable to university studies. He was Alexander of Hales, born about 1175, who thus founded in 1231 the Franciscan school in Paris, which he made famous by his own writings and by the pupils whom he taught there and who succeeded him in his chair: Jean de la Rochelle, Eudes Rigaud, William of Meliton, and St Bonaventure.

It is on the last of these that we must dwell, both because of his own fame and for the evidence he provides on the trends in a great school of Christian thought in the middle of the thirteenth century. In these last few years there has been a great deal of argument over whether we should say that Bonaventure's thought was Neo-Platonic Aristotelianism or Augustinianism influenced by Aristotle, whether it belongs to the field of philosophy or that of theology. Each of these judgements can be supported by serious arguments, which nevertheless do nothing to diminish the weight of those to the contrary. We can surely include all in a synthesis which preserves that part of the truth which each contains, and say that St Bonaventure's system represents one of the finest and highest examples of Christian philosophy. True, St Bonaventure makes room for many Aristotelian ideas: act and potency, matter and form, substance and accident, abstraction, the distinction between the active and the possible intellects, the idea of the soul as the form of the body. Nonetheless, he very firmly rejects the system as a whole (cf. *Collationes in Hexaemeron* VI, 2–5; written in 1270) because, in his eyes, it is fundamentally vitiated by its denial of exemplary Ideas in God and of Providence, and by its affirmation of the eternity of the world and the unity of the intellect, which undermines free will and personal immortality. In the essential points where faith incorporates a philosophy, St Bonaventure took care that Platonism should have a certain predominance. If indeed we must mix the water of philosophy with the wine of theology, we must be careful not to change the wine into water (*Coll. in Hex.*, VII, 14).

So for the Franciscan master the first teaching of Christian wisdom consists in the assertion of exemplarism. God has formed in himself the Idea of every species, of every created thing. He realized them by creating the beings of this world according to the archetypes in himself (*rationes aeternae*). Created things are only the reflection of the divine thought. It can be seen that this is a very simple and grand conception of the world, in which to the Biblical idea of the omnipotence of God is added the Greeks' love of wisdom and intelligence. It is thus possible for St Bonaventure to hold a theory of knowledge strictly parallel to his metaphysics. Man knows created things because, as he perceives them, he discovers the divine

Idea in God. But he can only give eternal or absolute value to his ideas or judgements by taking them back to their source in God. By the divine illumination God gives to every man, the eternal Ideas are both the efficient cause and the object of our knowing. Doubtless our knowledge of these Ideas is less clear than that which will be granted to us in eternal life, but the light is still the same in its nature, even if our eyes are too be-fogged by the sin of Adam and the condition of the flesh to see it in all its splendour. The words of Psalm 35, "in thy light shall we see light", are interpreted as in the myth of the cave in Plato's *Republic*: men see on the wall of the cave in which they are chained the shadows cast by the sun as things pass before the entrance of their prison.

But we can see that St Bonaventure modifies what is ex-cessive in Greek intellectualism, by teaching an intuition of moral values analogous to intellectual illumination. Alongside of conscience, which knows spontaneously and infallibly, in the sphere of action of the practical intellect, the basic moral values, he lays emphasis on *synderesis*, which instinctively, as it were, impels us towards the good and protests against moral failing. This image of God in us is clearly supernatural: it is in a category above all philosophical morality, as the Franciscan doctor never ceases to remind us, because the latter is ignorant of the true end of life and of the means of attaining to it in the light of grace.

It is not possible to set out in detail here the whole of St Bonaventure's system, still less to analyse the very different teachings of the various schools of Franciscan thought. But at least let us remark on a few essential common characteristics.

Generally speaking, the medieval Franciscans maintained a very close union between philosophy and theology. Without denying the difference between their methods, they held that a pure philosophy, perfectly independent of a theology to com-plete it, was impossible.

They were less sure than other Aristotelians that the soul was the form of the body. A remnant of Platonism made them attribute to the soul a greater freedom from the body. What is more, for them the soul was really identical with its faculties; the real distinction taught by St Thomas was rejected. So, to explain the action of the body, which thus depends less strictly on the soul, Franciscan Augustinianism was logically led to affirm the plurality of forms: beside the spiritual form are the animal form and the form of the vegetative life.

Among the faculties the will, or the emotive faculty in general, claims the primacy. Love is more important than knowledge and makes a man richer. In knowledge itself, the divine illumination, intuition, the sense of the concrete, took precedence. Abstractionism was not favoured: Franciscan masters continually appealed away from it to the personal experience of the interior life and to the direct experience which puts the soul in immediate contact with objects more effectively than concepts can do.

Thus, we can see that Aristotelianism could exist in such systems on the whole periphery of Christian philosophy. It could provide an explanation of the world and, in part, of man. But it could never be more than material to be worked over again and assimilated in a spirit that was not its own.

ST THOMAS AND SIGER OF BRABANT

The Dominicans had also obtained a footing in the faculty of theology in Paris about 1230. For a long time they were viewed with suspicion by the other masters for having refused to make common cause with them in the great strike of the schools. Their first masters did not shine very brilliantly, and taught a conservative Augustinianism. But two foreign masters suddenly brought their school incomparable splendour, and opened up new paths to Christian thought: a Swabian, Albertus Magnus, who taught from 1240 to 1248, and then an Italian, Thomas Aquinas, from 1252 to 1259 and again from 1269 to 1272. Neither of them had any scruple in accepting the influence of Aristotle, and they succeeded in establishing a Christian interpretation of his system.

The first characteristic of the system of Albert and St Thomas is their willingness to grant philosophy a new autonomy and independence. Even in its fallen state, as a result of original sin, man's reason is able to discover some truths about God and man and the world. The proof is that Aristotle set forth a coherent system, many ideas in which correspond to natural truths contained in revelation. Other truths can be called "revealable", in the sense that God could have taught them to men if he had not thought it better that they should discover them for themselves. It is because these truths are revealable that the theologian can deal with them without leaving the field of his own competence. He often finds in them the way to a better understanding of the mysteries. By this means philosophy is set in a Christian context but is no longer intrinsically religious. St Thomas never taught philosophy, for he was always a professor of theology, but he was certainly aware of the possibility of an autonomous use of reason for which the faith was no more than an external criterion. He himself gave very little time to this work, although his commentaries on Aristotle are among the most penetrating and have often provided material for reflection, or were even used as textbooks in the arts faculty. But most of the time St Thomas speaks of philosophical topics when dealing with faith. He requires philosophy to extend and clarify theology, as we can see in the *Summa theologiae*.

Obviously he had to face many objections in defending Aristotle, some of whose ideas, as we have said, are anti-Christian. He replied firmly to his adversaries that the Greek philosopher has often been slandered and misjudged in the light of commentators who played him false. What is more, an acceptable meaning can be given to many Aristotelian ideas. The philosopher taught that the world existed from all eternity. This is untrue, for the Bible tells us that God created all things in time. Yet it remains true that God could have created from all eternity, for the contingence of creation rests not so much in its temporal character as in its causal dependence. Modern scholars may not always agree with St Thomas's judgement on the precise meaning of Aristotle's ideas. He knew less history than we do. But the philosophical genius of Aquinas is not thereby lessened. On the contrary, it appears in the transplanting of ideas and in the power with which they were re-thought. In proportion as the real Aristotle appears different from what St Thomas supposed him to be, the originality of the latter shines out. This would be a serious matter had St Thomas wanted to teach the history of philosophy. But it is an additional merit if we take him for what he was, a thinker, a theologian, a philosopher. In any case it is the fact that Aristotle provided St Thomas with ideas essential to his system, such as the transcendentals and the analogy of being; the metaphysical composition of created things as act and potency, matter and form, substance and accidents; the primacy of act over potency; matter as the principle of individuation; the identity of each pure intelligence with its species; the impossibility of an infinite causal regress; and the proofs for the existence of a first being.

How can we sum up here a teaching so rich in its content? It will no doubt be better to concern ourselves with essentials, without encumbering ourselves with details which can be found in any manual of Thomist philosophy.

In the field of epistemology, we must first of all mark St Thomas's confidence in the human mind. It finds itself faced by a reality that is truly substantial, that is not simply a reflection or a shadow. It is to glorify God, to recognize that reality exists for itself and in itself, although it subsists only by its relation of dependence on the supreme being. But this dependence in no way limits its value.

And precisely because these lower, sensible things really do exist, they are what we ought to study in themselves, without turning away from them towards a divine source and waiting for the light. St Thomas thus finds himself as deprived of an *a priori* in studying these things as the empiricist Aristotle, relying only on his own observation to pierce to the truth of them.

The human mind is endowed with all that it needs to know created things, it has in itself a spiritual power of abstraction, the active intellect. St Thomas thus separates himself as much from Averroes as from St Bonaventure. He denies that there could be a single, unique intellect for the whole species. In each of us the soul is a spiritual faculty of knowing and of free will. The ambiguous quotations from Aristotle which the Arabian commentator uses for his own purposes St Thomas thus interprets in quite a different way. As for the doctrine of illumination, it seems to St Thomas, all things considered, less significant for the glory of God than might at first appear. Instead of God's intervening at every instant in all our knowing, is it not better that he should have given man all the powers needed for intellectual knowledge? The personal intellect must be capable of seizing the necessary and metaphysical aspect contained in the datum which the internal and external senses have presented. This active intellect abstracts the concept and communicates it to the passive intellect, which takes possession of it.

This concern to put the conditions of its existence within the thing itself was to determine the whole of the Thomist metaphysics and give a more profound meaning to the distinction between essence and existence of which Boëthius and Avicenna had already had something to say. Aristotle rightly said that being is essentially perfection and act. Yet the beings which we see are far from perfect; they begin in time and are limited in their worth. This is because in them the act (their *existence*) has been limited by a precise determination which makes them exist in a relative and incomplete manner. Their *essence* does not cover all the potentialities of being. Among all its limitations one is particularly radical, that by which it exists in space and time, in divisibility and multiplicity. So we shall say that the *form* of such beings is not pure like that of an angel, but is affected by a mark of metaphysical inferiority, by *matter*. Finite being is thus constituted as such by its formal essence. It is not inertia but activity, so that it is a source of values, or acquires them. It is at once stable and permanent, the subject of attributes, a *substance*, and susceptible of a new kind of being, an *accident*, something added to what it already was or had.

It might seem that such an accumulation of metaphysical

compositions greatly diminishes the value of contingent and corporeal being. But what do they do but express the interior wealth of a being which, though curbed and limited, is nonetheless an act analogous to the first act which is God? St Thomas's contemporaries made no mistake about it, but saw in this metaphysics an attempt to establish and justify an intrinsic autonomy in existent things, which were no longer only reflections of God but real centres of subsistence and activity. The idea of nature, clarified and expressed with such difficulty in the twelfth century, here finds its complete justification. The theory of the four causes emphasizes its fundamental rôle in a striking way, for the form acts in a clearly determined fashion to obtain certain effects in conformity with the good of the nature (formal cause); realizing itself outwardly, it produces its effects (efficient cause) in view of an end (final cause), and in a way shapes things (material cause) according to its instinct or will. It would be untrue to say that the world thus analysed by St Thomas was estranged from God: it depends on him, in fact, completely and utterly, by the relation of creation. But since Aquinas found this account of the world in an author who knew nothing of this relation of dependence, he was the more tempted to explain the world for and in itself and to give it an autonomy which, if secondary, is none the less real.

Moreover, St Thomas in some sort forces Aristotelianism to recognize this God, by proving his existence and his providence from the essential principles of the system itself. Taking as his starting-point the texts in Aristotle's *Physics* demonstrating the existence of a prime mover, St Thomas gives a quite new breadth to the argument. For movement is a transition from potency to act. It can only occur because of the action of a being, an act, and as we cannot go on *ad infinitum* in a causal series we must end by postulating the existence of a subsistent being, pure act, first cause, first in the order of the good, of the true, and of being. Since beings exist apart from God, they must have been created by him, for a being which has not its existence of itself can only have received it.

None of these beings which inhabit the world is comparable to man in nobility. St Thomas, who retained the Neo-Platonist idea of hierarchical order, recalls—frequently indeed—that man stands at the intersection of the world of the spirit and the world of matter, for he has a soul and a body. St Thomas interpreted this duality better than any other Christian writer, by affirming at the same time that the human soul is a substance and that it is the form of the body.

The human soul must be substantial, since it possesses wholly spiritual faculties such as thought and free will. It is therefore spiritual and quite free from matter, and can subsist in itself apart from the body. What Aristotle granted only hypothetically in this regard, St Thomas affirms categorically. But he had no intention of cutting himself off from the Aristotelian idea of the soul as the form of the body. For normally the soul uses the body as an instrument: this indeed is why it will joyfully find the body again in the future life, but obviously in a more glorious state.

In the present life, despite the servitude of this condition of the flesh, the body is not at all the tomb, the prison of the soul, that Plato spoke of. Its experience, its information, is drawn from sense impressions, just as the will is stimulated and invigorated by the emotions. So there is brought into being an intimate collaboration. That which subsists is man; not the soul alone, but the soul communicating its substantiality to the body and conscious of it directly even in its least spiritual activity. There is thus no reason to postulate the existence of subordinate forms, nor to fear for the independence of the soul. What the soul itself cannot directly do in the material world is possible to it if it can use a means of action intimately united to it. In the same way, what thinks in a man is not the soul alone, but the man as a whole, because he is endowed with a reasonable soul. Entirely devoid of innate ideas, and without divine illumination, the soul can only know things if the sensible object come to it through the organic senses. It is on what they provide it with that the soul exercises its powers, abstracting the idea from the brute fact.

Although St Thomas gave such a warm and generous welcome to Aristotelianism, it was not enough for some professors of the arts faculty in Paris: Siger of Brabant, Boëthius of Dacia, Bernier of Nivelles and others wanted more. They have often been called Averroists, because they wanted to follow faithfully that Arabic philosopher's interpretation. If the epithet is perhaps too strong, their position is nonetheless very similar to that of Averroes, and they do preserve at least some of his ideas, such as the unity of the intellect for the whole human species, the eternity of the world, the denial of Providence and of human freedom. These theses above all were aimed at by the condemnations pronounced in 1270 and 1277 by Stephen Tempier, the Bishop of Paris.

The spirit of these arts teachers was certainly Averroist in the sense that like their master they have no concern for faith or theology. It would be untrue to say, as has sometimes been said, that they taught the doctrine of two kinds of truth, one in theology and another in philosophy. Whenever there is an opposition between these two, Siger always asserts that he sides with the faith, that the reason may make mistakes and ought to bow therefore before a higher kind of knowledge. But he nevertheless went on teaching heterodox ideas, declaring that the rôle of a professor of philosophy is not to seek out and lay down the truth but to echo faithfully the teaching of the great philosophers. Who can sift out from such an attitude what is merely evasive and what is good faith?

Besides, it was certainly an Averroist Aristotelianism that Siger and his followers taught. God, the first being, created of necessity the first Intelligence. From all eternity this process of emanation goes on until we reach a last, separate intelligence which rules the sublunary world and there plays the part of intellect: the possible intellect and the active intellect for the human species. Man is thus a higher animal who is, by a special privilege, in close contact with the soul of the world. His senses provide images from which this soul draws general concepts. So his activity is ours in a certain sense. But it does not last for ever, for only the common soul is immortal.

Clearly such theses could not but provoke lively opposition: it came from St Bonaventure, St Albertus Magnus and St Thomas. St Thomas's was the most effective by far, for his criticism came from within the movement: he wrote not only as a carefully orthodox theologian, but as an Aristotelian, disputing the propriety of the proposed interpretations. Because of this criticism Siger of Brabant modified his ideas considerably and thus came nearer to Christian Aristotelianism. But his system, though condemned, as we have said, could still be revived even in Paris, by John of Jandun, and in Italy, at Padua.

CHAPTER V

THE END OF THE MIDDLE AGES

To bring together writers like Siger of Brabant and John of Jandun, though they are indeed joined in a common philosophical attitude, is to evoke the whole difference in style and method which separates the thirteenth from the fourteenth century. Siger was a concise writer, a precise thinker who went straight to essentials, and who even with his great intellectual curiosity knew certain bounds of discretion. John of Jandun was prolix and difficult, afraid of no abstruse subtlety. However small the question might be, it produced from him interminable commentaries and distinctions. And as much might be said of his contemporaries. The scholasticism of the fourteenth and fifteenth centuries grew extraordinarily heavy and dull. It seemed to have lost all contact with reality or with its sources. It argued and quibbled and complicated everything. Logic it both used and abused.

And the spirit of the age turned towards criticism and polemical argument. When the great masters left the scene, let us say for simplicity's sake about 1280, their pupils systematized their teachings and codified them, and defended them in a sectarian spirit that replaced the more profound inspiration of the earlier period. Their fondness for accusations and *correctoria* is a contrast to the friendship and respect that characterized the relations between those two geniuses St Bonaventure and St Thomas Aquinas.

Everything was called in question, first and foremost the authority of Aristotle.

But let us be careful not to think that this last period of the Middle Ages knew no great philosophers. On the contrary, there were two who must be introduced here at least briefly, the English Franciscans, Duns Scotus and William of Ockham.

DUNS SCOTUS

Born at Maxton in Scotland about 1265, John Duns entered the Franciscan order towards 1278. After his years as a student at Oxford and at Cambridge, he taught as bachelor *Sententiarum* in Paris in 1302 and at Oxford in 1303 and 1304. Returning to Paris, he became master of theology and taught there as master before going in the same capacity to Cologne, where he died on November 8th, 1308.

Duns Scotus is known for his dialectical power and for the profundity of his teaching, by his proposal to analyse "essences" and to base his teaching on this analysis. Has he not been given the title of "the Subtle Doctor"? Yet he is clearly withdrawing from the position of St Thomas: he has less confidence than the latter in the powers of the reason or in the orthodoxy of Aristotle. The critics of Averroism had done their work. Duns Scotus considered, in particular, that the Greek philosopher did not teach that God was Providence nor that the human soul was spiritual and immortal. Since at that time philosophy was more or less identified with "the philosopher" of Stagira, the Franciscan master maintained that philosophy could not prove these two doctrines. And there were others besides which, according to Duns Scotus, men had wrongly tried to prove by the reason, for example that God is omnipotent, infinite, true, just and merciful. These are truths which Duns Scotus reserves strictly to faith and revelation, not only from a historical point of view, because no philosopher perceived them, but absolutely, because they cannot be demonstrated. As for the other attributes of God, they are only philosophically demonstrable by their effects (*a posteriori*), while the only proofs worthy of the name are *a priori*, those which give the fundamental reason for the fact thus established. To meet these intellectual requirements, Duns Scotus restricted the field of philosophical inquiry and separated it from theology more strictly than had been done in the thirteenth century. This latter discipline was a matter of authority, and used to a less extent arguments of general plausibility (*convenientia*). The vast area which St Thomas held as common to philosophy and theology, that of those natural truths which faith has revealed or could have revealed (*revelabilia*), was split in two, into that of the truths of faith (*credibilia*) and that of philosophical truths. Nothing that is demonstrable by the reason has been revealed by God, and nothing that has been revealed by God is demonstrable by the reason. The action of Providence in the history of the world and in our lives, the precepts of his law, all this is impenetrable. This is the field, no longer of the divine reason, where our reason, according to St Thomas, can still see something, but of the divine will. This is one of the aspects of that Scotist voluntarism which also appears in his conception of theology as a science more practical than theoretical, and which was to end in Ockham with the assertion of a kind of divine arbitrariness.

It is extremely difficult to set out briefly the essential ideas of Scotism. On the one hand, editions of his works are often wanting, and the authenticity of more than one of them is still in question. For this reason the remarkable editorial work undertaken by Fr Balič and his colleagues will be welcomed with the more warmth. On the other hand, there seems to have been a kind of tension in the thought of Scotus himself, between points of view that were diverse, or at least complementary of one another rather than systematized.

This can be seen clearly, for example, in his epistemological and metaphysical teaching. On the one hand, Scotus asserts with Aristotle and St Thomas that all human knowledge has its origins in the senses and is built up by abstraction. On the other, he holds that the object of the intelligence is not the material object but the intelligible being, a universal, univocal property that the divine illumination has deposited innately, as it were, in us. The reconciliation of these two doctrines is found by recourse to original sin, which altered the conditions of human nature and lessened the power of the intellect. Hence this curious mixture of the idea of abstraction, which leads to empiricism, with that of innate ideas, which emphasizes the importance of the universal concept (conceptualism). To the idea which exists in us as a concept "of second intention" corresponds in reality a "common nature", with a mark of individuality intrinsic to the form itself. This man is by the same principle "this" and "man". He is not individualized by matter but by a concrete determination, the *haecceitas*. In one sense he is nearer to the universal essence, which he wholly reproduces, but in another he himself has greater importance than in classical Aristotelianism.

There seems to be the same indecision in the proofs for the existence of God. For on the one side, as we have seen, Scotus severely censures attempts at a natural theology, yet on the other he wants to establish philosophically the existence of an infinite God. Does he contradict himself? No; for, as Etienne Gilson has shown, he followed the tradition of St Anselm and had no hesitation in borrowing from faith the very notions which were to be the foundation of his argument.

The first part of the proof starts from the idea that certain beings could be produced. Not, be it noted, from the contingent fact that certain beings may have been made, but from the absolute and undeniable assertion of the possibility of creation. We do not have to observe a fact, but to intuit an essence. And if a created essence is possible, so too is a creator. Now if a first cause is possible, it exists.

Why? It is here that the second stage of the proof begins. This first, possible cause could only be infinite in its perfection. Its efficient causality affects all things, it knows all possibilities, it is the final cause of all things, and it above all realizes the perfection of being. So it is enough to state this to conclude: a possible infinite being can only be real because if it remains only possible it is no longer infinite. There would be a being more perfect than it, that which is infinite and real. The possible infinite being would lack one part of its perfection, that of existence; and this is a contradiction.

WILLIAM OF OCKHAM

Ockham was born at the end of the thirteenth century and entered the Franciscan order about 1310. He first studied and then taught at Oxford. Having become a bachelor *Sententiarum* he was about to receive his doctorate when in 1324 he was summoned to appear before the pope at Avignon. Hence the title of *Inceptor* (candidate for a doctorate) which was given him by tradition, to which *venerabilis* was added by his followers. He had been denounced to the pope by the chancellor of Oxford, and had to reply about various heretical or erroneous propositions extracted from his commentary on the *Sentences*. In the pontifical city of Avignon he also became involved in the dispute over the "evangelical poverty" which some members of his order wanted imposed with absolute strictness. Before either of these processes had been completed, Ockham fled from Avignon with the general of the order to the camp of the emperor, Louis the Bavarian, who was in open conflict with the pope. That was in 1328, and for twenty years Ockham was to keep up the fight against the papal power, along with Marsilius of Padua. He died at Munich of the Black Death a little later than the emperor, in 1349—just as, it seems, he was seeking reconciliation with the pope.

In a sense, we can say that Ockham's system is a protest against the philosophy of essences, primarily as it is expressed in Scotus' "essentialist metaphysics", but also as in the "realism" of St Thomas or the school of Chartres.

Even in the field of logic Ockham had but one fundamental principle: "only individuals exist", and he drew from this all its consequences. Among men, there is Socrates, or there is Plato. They are like one another, it is true, but Socrates is no more Plato than Plato is Socrates. There is no human nature or essence common to Socrates and Plato in which they might be harmoniously united. Yet the essence that is Socrates and that which is Plato are alike: this is what makes it possible to call them by a common name. The concept can only be a product of the mind, useful no doubt in practice but hardly having any foundation in fact, by which we sum up in our limited intelligence the resemblances perceived between things. As can be seen, Ockham applies to all concepts what we might say of this or that hasty or unfounded generalization. By way of illustration we may refer to what was said at the beginning of this book, that the thinkers of the Middle Ages do not make up a homogeneous group but must be split into several groups or movements, which it would be useless to try to cover with one collective name, invented by those who dislike them so as to make it easier to exclude them from the history of thought.

Ockham's logical theories had a metaphysical aspect; we have already noticed the same development in similar cases. In fact, his criticism was no less relevant to the theory of divine ideas which underlay realism than to logical "realism". Indeed, many authors, as we have seen, in order to justify the existence of genera and the natures which they expressed, said that our concepts merely reflected more or less exactly the Ideas which are in God. This was a conjunction, as we have remarked, of the Platonic notion of separate Ideas and the Christian notion of a good and wise God who creates all things according to a plan, an intellectual model or pattern of the creation. This notion could be set out from the side of God, as we saw with St Bonaventure: then one would say that human ideas are communicated to us by the divine illumination, which, on the logical level, is analogous to the exemplarism which governed all the work of the creation. But it could also be presented from the side of creatures, as in St Thomas: then one speaks first of natures, and from them one ascends both towards God the creator and towards the human mind which knows the divine plan from its actualization in the creation.

For Ockham, both these ways of looking at things are necessarily false, because they allow Greek philosophy to permeate our view of the world. It was Plato who spoke of Ideas, Aristotle who emphasized natures. Now all this, and especially Aristotelianism, imposes an arbitrary limitation on the divine omnipotence and freedom. God cannot be limited by natures, which would be independent of him, nor even by Ideas, which would be before him or in him. God is uncaused action, freedom; he made things, and forms and rules, without consulting any "reason", personal or impersonal.

All this is of major importance in determining Ockham's metaphysics. For Ockham, there is no longer any necessity to reconstruct or re-think the world beginning from non-existent essences or abstract principles: *entia non sunt multiplicanda sine necessitate* is his phrase—Ockham's razor, as it has been wittily called. We cannot know *a priori* what God has willed, because he wills without following any rule. We have to look at things and see into them by a direct experience, by intuition. Ockham thus turns his back on all his predecessors, who saw in things, alongside of the essence, the obscure zone of individuality. It is the individuality itself that Ockham claims to know with a knowledge of what it is in its concrete existence.

We have to be very careful about historical comparisons in these matters and use them cautiously if at all. Yet there is a real and curious analogy between Sartre's and Ockham's denial of essences, in their desire to get back to the concrete individual, and in their refusal to base their ethics on the nature of man. There is, however, a world of difference between the modern existentialists and Ockham. Ockham looked to theology for what he could not prove or explain in philosophy. If we can say that there is a certain order in the world, it is because revelation has declared it to us. We are thus justified in studying it, not according to *a priori* principles, but quite prosaically by studying concrete existents. It is indeed in this sense that we ought to understand the oft-repeated assertion that Ockham is the father of modern science, although it is forgotten, when that is said, that some Franciscan philosophers of the thirteenth century, like Grosseteste and Roger Bacon, or an Aristotelian like St Albertus Magnus, achieved much of value in scientific research. Still, it is true that by putting first the intuitive knowledge of the concrete individual, and by demanding a carefully detailed examination of the facts, Ockham prepared men's minds for the requirements of the experimental method. The logical rules which he established for discovering and describing causes, and his insistence on the need to vary the antecedent factors of phenomena, remind one of the logic of science worked out by Francis Bacon and by John Stuart Mill.

In ethics, Ockham could have been led logically into the most complete indifferentism, for according to him the human will is not determined in any way; it is not directed towards the supreme good. What is more, what is good for one man may be bad for another, because there is no essence of man. No act is intrinsically good or evil, not even in the eyes of God; for if the contrary were true, God would not be free in laying down his law. Nevertheless, Ockham managed to establish a theory of morality, by referring to revelation. It is God's will that we should act in such and such a manner. But this is perfectly arbitrary: he could just as well have commanded us to hate as to love, have made adultery right and trustworthiness wrong. Right and wrong are therefore never founded in reason; they depend solely on the free choice of God. It follows that, to act rightly, a man should not act through love of virtue or of the good. These do not exist, strictly speaking. We can only be morally good if we obey a law, and do it with the will to obey.

Ockham's ethics is thus one of pure obligation, of positive obligation. It was no accident that Ockham's followers tended to confuse law and morality, turning their backs on an ethics of charity and the virtues.

After this, it is somewhat surprising to find Ockham speaking of natural law, since for him there is no essence of nature, and if one did exist it would have to be orientated to a certain good, apart from all positive obligation. Some have seen in this the possibility of a contradiction in Ockham's thought, but perhaps we need not go so far as that. For the English friar distinguishes what God wills by his absolute power, or *absolutely*, from what he prescribes in his ordering of the creation, *ordinatione*. Absolutely, God commands whatever he wills; for him there is no moral evil. But in ordering his creation, God chose a moral order which, once arbitrarily established, has its own logic and its own requirements. Now on this hypothesis, God wills that we should obey the suggestions of our reason.

This is not a matter of aspiration or of tendency towards the good, but simply of a precisely established order. If a man acted without actually wanting to obey this ordering he would not be morally right. As for the content of this natural law, it would clearly be useless to look for it by analysing human inclinations. We must look to experience, for only experience shows that some actions are good for society in general while others destroy it.

CONCLUSION

How can we conclude this book? Must we sum up the essential lines of development, when we have already had to summarize ideas and facts? Perhaps it is better to introduce very briefly a man—and I say a man rather than an author quite naturally, because here the system depends above all on the personality —who can best symbolize the transition from the Middle Ages to the Renaissance: Nicholas of Cusa.

He was of the Middle Ages in the way in which he fought for the ecclesiastical against the lay power, against Sigismond, the Duke of Tyrol, from whom he wished to recover the goods belonging to his bishopric of Brixen. But he was clearly no longer medieval when, for a short time at any rate, he took the side of the council of Basle against Eugenius IV; how far this is from Innocent III! He was medieval again in his way of philosophizing in a Christian context and spirit, with his respect for older authorities. But when he prefers Dionysius and Plotinus to Aristotle he reminds us more of the sixteenth century than the thirteenth or fourteenth. His devotion to the classics, and his quest for manuscripts—it was he who found the complete text of Plautus' comedies in a Rhenish library— certainly remind us of the keenness of the scholars of twelfth century Chartres, but his zeal was too exclusive, too enthusiastic, not to make him seem like a man of the Renaissance. This indeed is what he was, this son of the Moselle boatmen, born in 1401 at Cues near Trier, pupil of the Brethren of the Common Life and of the universities of Heidelberg and Padua, an indefatigable jurist, an experienced and wise administrator, who was to work for the union of the Churches during the Council of Florence and end his life on August 15th, 1464, as cardinal and papal legate.

Nicholas's thought is perhaps less interesting for his ideas, which can all be found in many other writers, than for the general trend of his writing, its methods and its spirit. He was not an Ockhamist, and thought, for example, that universals exist both in a "straitened" manner in individuals and in a formal manner in the divine Word. Yet he was affected by the scepticism of his time and by the criticisms of the great syntheses of the thirteenth century. He did not deny the value of the rational intelligence, but preferred to it as ways of knowing, intuition, symbolism and love. This was essentially what he called "wise ignorance" (*docta ignorantia*). This is a very Socratic notion, for it is a question of being aware of the limits of knowledge in a clear and courageous way. We can no more perfectly know God or the truth of things than a polygon inscribed in a circle can perfectly coincide with it. Knowledge is relative, complex, finite, always perfectible; but truth is absolute, simple and one.

One ... this is the characteristic of truth and reality that Nicholas of Cusa insisted on most. Faced by the contradiction of ideas and facts, his mind sought always the higher unity, the synthesis which surpasses differences. God is the *coincidentia oppositorum*, at once infinitely great and infinitely small. He transcends the contradictions and distinctions of creatures and unites them in himself in a way beyond our understanding, of which only the negative theology can speak. God contains all things, he is *omnia complicans*, but he is also the source of the multitude of things which reveal something of himself, *omnia explicans*. Each thing reflects the whole universe, which in one sense is infinite and could contain many other worlds besides our own. There is in this cosmic aspect of each thing a clear foreshadowing of the monadology of Leibniz. But still more clearly man "contracts" within himself every element, every mode of being: he is the microcosmic image of the macrocosm.

At the risk of oversimplification, we could say that Nicholas uses all the elements of medieval thought in the service of a wider synthesis. For he realized, better than the men of the two centuries before him, that the medieval world was too narrow, too "contracted", to use his own word. But if it was true that man was beginning to see himself as more important, if it was true that the world was suddenly to expand through geographical and scientific discovery, nevertheless it was still true that the Middle Ages had done justice to the universality of God and his Providence. So he safeguarded in very difficult times and hard—we too easily forget this—the "one thing necessary". It is paradoxical that he should bear witness of this to us, who now, in a world which has shrunk to a tiny planet among many in an infinite universe, run the risk of forgetting that true riches lie in man's discourse with God. We always come back to the same thing: Christian Socratism, Christian philosophy.

SELECT BIBLIOGRAPHY

AQUINAS, St Thomas: *Basic Writings of St Thomas Aquinas*, edited by Anton C. Pegis, New York, Random House, and London, Burns Oates, 1945.

AUGUSTINE, St: *Basic Writings of St Augustine*, edited by Whitney J. Oates, two volumes, New York, Random House, 1948.

BARRETT, H. M.: *Boethius*, Cambridge and New York, Cambridge Univ. Press, 1940.

BETT, H.: *John Scotus Erigena*, Cambridge and New York, Cambridge Univ. Press, 1925.

COPLESTON, F. C., S.J.: *A History of Philosophy* (vol. 2, St Augustine to Duns Scotus; vol. 3, Ockham to Suarez), London, Burns Oates, and Westminster, Md, Newman Press, 1950, 1953; *Aquinas*, London and Baltimore, Penguin Books, 1955.

CROMBIE, A. C.: *Robert Grosseteste and the Origins of Experimental Science, 1100–1700*, Oxford and New York, Oxford Univ. Press, 1953.

D'ARCY, M., S.J., and others: *A Monument to St Augustine*, London and New York, Sheed and Ward, 1930.

DE BOER, T.: *History of Philosophy in Islam*, Stuttgart, 1901, trans. E. Jones, London, 1903.

DE WULF, M.: *History of Mediaeval Philosophy*, 3rd English edn. translated by Ernest C. Messenger, two volumes, London, Longmans, 1935, 1938; 4th English edn., also translated by Ernest C. Messenger, vol. 1, London, Nelson, and (3 volumes) New York, Dover Publications, 1952.

GILSON, E.: *A History of Christian Philosophy in the Middle Ages*, London and New York, Sheed and Ward, 1955; *The Spirit of Medieval Philosophy*, translated by A. H. C. Downes, London and New York, Sheed and Ward, 1936; *The Mystical Theology of St Bernard*, translated by A. H. C. Downes, London and New York, Sheed and Ward, 1940; *The Philosophy of St Bonaventure*, translated by Dom Illtyd Trethowan and F. J. Sheed, London and New York, Sheed and Ward, 1948.

HAWKINS, D. J. B.: *A Sketch of Mediaeval Philosophy*, London and New York, Sheed and Ward, 1947.

HUSIK, I.: *Medieval Jewish Philosophy*, New York, Macmillan, 1916.

LEFF, G.: *Medieval Thought from St Augustine to Ockham*, London and Baltimore, Penguin Books, 1958.

MCKEON, Richard: *Selections from Medieval Philosophers*, two volumes, New York, Scribner, 1929.

RASHDALL, J. H.: *Medieval Universities*, Volume I revised by F. M. Powicke and A. B. Emden, Oxford, and New York, Oxford Univ. Press, 1936.

TAYLOR, H. O.: *The Medieval Mind*, New York, Macmillan, 1927.

VAN STEENBERGHEN, J.: *Aristotle in the West*, translated by L. Johnston, Louvain, 1955; *The Philosophical Movement in the Thirteenth Century*, London and New York, Nelson, 1955.

The Twentieth Century Encyclopedia
of Catholicism

*The number of each volume indicates its place in
the over-all series and not the order of publication.*

TWENTIETH CENTURY ENCYCLOPEDIA OF CATHOLICISM

All titles are subject to change.